CLARISSA DICKSON WRIGHT AND JENNIFER PATERSON

TWO FAT LADIES
OBSESSIONS

press
élan

A GENERAL PUBLISHING IMPRINT

FOR

PATRICIA LLEWELLYN whose vision launched us onto the world, introduced us to all of you, our new friends of the past four years, and gave us a voice so that you could learn of our obsessions and our philosophies and perhaps walk with us along this path.

ACKNOWLEDGMENTS

We both want to thank all the producers, farmers and shops who have fought against the demons of Europe and bureaucracy to bring us proper food.

We also want to thank our 'fan', HRH the Prince of Wales for all he did to keep the small flame of the organic movement alive in the dark ages so that we could all benefit now.

NOTE: Unless otherwise indicated all recipes serve 4–6

This edition published in Great Britain in 1999

1 3 5 7 9 10 8 6 4 2

Copyright © Optomen Television and Jennifer Paterson and Clarissa Dickson Wright 1999

Jennifer Paterson and Clarissa Dickson Wright have asserted their moral right to be identified as the authors of this work under the Copyright, Designs and Patent Act 1988

First published in Canada 1999 by élan press, an imprint of
General Publishing Co, 30 Lesmill Road
Toronto, Ontario
Canada M3E 2T6

First published in the United Kingdom in 1999 by Ebury
Press, Random House
Vauxhall Bridge Road, London SW1V 2SA

Canadian Cataloguing in Publication data

Paterson, Jennifer
Two Fat Ladies: Obsessions

ISBN 1-55144-233-7

1.   Cookery, British   I. Wright, Clarissa Dickson II.
Title

TX717.P375 1999   641.5941   C99-931712-1

Food photography by Laurie Evans
Food styling by Pete Smith
Styling by Lesley Richardson
Design by Senate
Artwork by Essential Books
Illustrations for chapters 2, 4, 5, 7, 8, 11, 12, 15, 17, 18, 20, 25 by Vivien Rothwell
Printed and bound in France

CONTENTS

PREFACE

'I think the Prince has poisoned me', Jennifer complained on the telephone on the morning of 30th June 1999. She had gone to bed early the night before, feeling exhausted after an exciting day at Highgrove, the Prince Of Wales' country home. This food writer's luncheon party was to be Jennifer's last social engagement. Over the next few days her condition deteriorated – her discomfort was clearly a sign of something more serious than poisoning by royal appointment.

After a series of tests at the Chelsea & Westminster Hospital the doctor came to tell Jennifer that she had cancer. In the manner of the modern NHS the doctor was accompanied by a counsellor. The doctor told Jennifer the news. The counsellor asked her gently if there was anything that she wanted. 'Yes,' she replied emphatically. 'A cigarette.'

Like her life, Jennifer's stay in hospital was filled with incidents such as this. Jennifer could always spontaneously come out with a memorable line, a phrase that anyone else would have had to spend months thinking about to perfect.

When the press found out she was ill journalists eager for a scoop attempted to get into her hospital room. For security reasons the hospital suggested we change her name on their computer and ward notice board. It was to be no plain Jane Smith for Jennifer. 'I've always wanted to be a Dame or a Lady' Jennifer told her friend David, Marquess of Queensberry. Between them they came up with the perfect moniker and minutes later it was written up on the notice board in green marker pen. And so it was that for the rest of her stay Jennifer was known as Lady Vita Circumference. In this, as in so many moments during Jennifer's time in hospital, I felt I was living in the midst of an Evelyn Waugh novel – an impression bolstered by the fridge in her room full of caviar sent by well-wishers after Jennifer complained her room was overflowing with flowers and she'd rather have something to eat instead of the 'disgusting' hospital food.

Jennifer was touched when Prince Charles sent her a vat of organic soup and ice cream from his private kitchens along with a hand-written note. She hugely enjoyed the food and it provoked a rediscovery of her youthful enthusiasm for ice cream. Once it was all gone it provided us with a difficult social conundrum. An etiquette teaser to stump even Debretts. What was the right way to deal with the Tupperware containers it had arrived in? Should she send them back or could she keep them?

In the first week of her stay in hospital Jennifer wasn't confined to her bed. She took pleasure in roaming the ward basking in her celebrity status. Jennifer was thrilled to find a 93-year old Reverend Mother in the next room but not half as thrilled as the nun was to meet Jennifer. 'Do get well soon', the nun insisted, somewhat urgently. 'We need you on television.' For days my head was full of visions of nuns clustered round the television watching *Two Fat Ladies*.

After only eight days in hospital Jennifer's condition took a rapid nose dive. Jennifer developed an infection and her weakened immune system was unable to fight it off. A priest was called and gave her the last rites. It seemed like the end. Then came a resurgence that I suspect was driven by Jennifer's passion for a good anecdote. (If you could only prescribe anecdotal recovery it would save the NHS a fortune.) Jennifer recovered in hours and was soon on the telephone proudly telling everyone 'I've had extra muncheon' – a Jenniferism for extreme unction. It cheered her up enormously. 'I'm in a state of grace dear' she would boast to visitors. (Imagine the mileage Lazarus must have got out of his story.)

Jennifer found diverse ways to amuse herself in her hospital bed. One of her favourites was to go through my make up bag, laughing at its range of lotions and potions. She admired my scissors and nail clippers but was horrified that anyone should buy make up from anywhere but Boots. Boots the chemist was her favourite shop and the only place she ever enjoyed shopping. It was Boots where she bought her favourite lipstick, a lurid orange called Gay Geranium that somehow looked fabulous on her. She was passionate about it, constantly trying to get people to try it on, something I had always managed to resist. From her hospital bed she tried again 'Do try it on. To please me,' she said. So I did. And spent the day looking like lamb dressed as dowager mutton.

Boots also provided her with the catarrh pastilles she would never leave home without. The principal task of these foul smelling lozenges was to ward off errant policemen who might stop her as she weaved along on her moped between drinks parties. Their pungent aroma could hide anything on the breath and guarantee that conversation was kept to an absolute minimum. Her interest in Boots was as girlie as Jennifer ever got. She had a handful of women friends but mostly she preferred the company of men. In 1997 the *Two Fat Ladies* won a Women In Film And Television award for creative ingenuity. After the prize giving an earnest young journalist asked Jennifer if she was proud to be sitting among all these successful women. 'Certainly not,' Jennifer replied instantly. 'I hate it. I'd much rather be sitting next to a man.'

Over the course of her four and a half weeks there, Jennifer's hospital bedroom became a kind of old-fashioned literary salon as friends came to call and were encouraged to drink, whatever time of the day or night. Jennifer was usually fastidious about her drinking: vodka before 3pm and whisky after 5.30pm (with a siesta in between), but hospital mealtimes played havoc with her Mediterranean habits. One morning I rang her at nine-thirty in the morning. Responding to my usual 'Still alive then?' (I learnt quickly that this was the best way to ask Jennifer how she was) she boomed into the phone 'I've got Beryl Bainbridge and Anna Haycroft [Alice Thomas Ellis] here, they're having a whisky.'

In life Jennifer refused to suffer fools gladly, and she saw no reason why illness should change that. One day, when a couple of friends and I were drinking champagne at her bedside, an unwelcome guest was announced. Jennifer shooed us into the bathroom to wait, stifling giggles while she feigned near unconsciousness, lying back and moaning loudly. As expected, the visitor left almost immediately. On another occasion I rang her and was shocked to hear her answer the phone in a pathetic little voice, far removed from the Jennifer I knew so well. 'Hello' she half whispered. 'Hello' I said, 'Still alive then?'. At this she instantly returned to her normal self, booming down the phone 'Oh it's you dear. Thank God, I thought it was another bloody do-gooder.'

Jennifer and I had joked for years that she'd probably die halfway through making the last *Two Fat Ladies* programme. I'd always teased her that I wouldn't allow her to stop the filming and would instead prop her up on the motorbike like Charlton Heston in the grand finale of *El Cid*. When she went into hospital we were halfway through the fourth series and had filmed four out of eight programmes but we hadn't recorded the crucial voice over for them. It was Jennifer who was determined that they should be finished and, propped up in bed and encouraged by Rex her much loved sound man, she gave the performance of a lifetime, waving away visitors and nurses with a haughty 'I'm recording for the BBC, you'll have to come back later.'

Jennifer's Catholic faith was very powerful and she was convinced that she was heading for a better place. 'None of my family has ever been scared of death,' she told me. Her conversations were peppered with tales of her beloved saints who she would call upon in any situation. In Australia I had a sore throat and she came back from mass with a pendant of St Blaise, who would heal me of this slight irritation. I didn't share her faith but this afternoon, thinking of Jennifer, I flicked through the Oxford Dictionary of Saints. Turning to the calendar at the back of the book I looked up August 10th, the day she died. It was the feast day of St Laurence. Patron saint of cooks.

Patricia Llewellyn
August 16th 1999

INTRODUCTION

I wrote this introduction for both of us. Jennifer became ill during the book's final stages and told me to get on with it as she was being pushed around by quacks. As you will probably know she died on 10 August, peacefully, painlessly and full of caviar. However, she would not have wanted this to detract from our message.

Anyone who has watched the programme over the last three years will know that one of the main things that binds us is an unswerving passion for good food - no compromises, no second best. You may have wondered to watch us going to such lengths to collect our own eggs, pick our own mussels or see the beef or pork on the hoof. Of course, in real life we don't always have the time but we wish to get across to you just how important real food and real ingredients are to us.

The title of this book, *Obsessions*, was chosen in part as a rude gesture to mimsy journalists who, content with GM adapted, irradiated, badly raised meat, reared without fat, suggest that we are obsessed. Perhaps we are, but anyone who has witnessed Jennifer's joy at the sight of 'a good little grouse bird', her enthusiasm for a sweetbread or my ecstasy at the sight of a cardoon will realise that it is a very fulfilling obsession.

My own contribution contains illegal substances. At the time of writing beef on the bone is still banned but I have written a section on it, and indeed on tripe, in the genuine belief that sometime in the future it will be returned to our tables.

Equally difficult to obtain is a good broad bean. Jennifer writes lovingly of them, yet they are invariably picked too old for sale in the shops and do not keep well. If you have any access to a little patch of land, grow broad beans on it.

Perforce this book also recognises our passions for different parts of the globe. Jennifer is a devout Italianist and anyone who was audience to her fury in the Cotswold Italian restaurant, which failed to produce even a pasta simpleci, will have no doubt of the purity of her devotion. On the way out the restaurateur offered us a plate of a well-known brand of chocolates, ''Ave a chocolate, I made them myself,' he cooed. Jennifer turned a withering gaze on him. 'In that case they are bound to be revolting,' she barked and swept out.

Jennifer spent several happy periods of her life in Italy, indeed her much loved father is buried in Venice. She talks with great pleasure about diving for sea urchins in Taormina with lithe young men and jokes about returning to visit them, now sitting in cafes, sporting the mustachios and striped suits of Mafia Dons.

For myself chilies and the ingredients of South East Asia constitute a good share of my enthusiasm (remember the word comes from 'entheos', meaning filled by the gods). My comfort food is Chinese and nothing cheers one up so much as a well-made wonton soup. My attempt to recreate the Chinese tripe dish I miss so much is, I suspect, as near to a search for Nirvana as I shall ever come.

We came to our 'obsession' with food by different routes. Jennifer claims her guide was greed; with the Second World War servants were unobtainable and her mother would have lived happily on a Cream Cracker and a brandy and seltzer. She liked food and therefore she had to cook it herself.

In my case I was bought up by a gourmet father and a mother who was a lavish hostess and cook. It was inevitable. My mother once said to a school friend of mine, 'I'm economising this month, darling, I shan't go to the Hilton for breakfast at all.' This was when the Hyde Park Hilton was new and the Roof Top Restaurant extremely good.

We are aided, abetted and encouraged in our obsession by our beloved director and producer Patricia Llewellyn, who grew up in her parents first class restaurant in New Castle, Emlyn. We all owe a great debt of gratitude to Mrs Llewellyn, her mother. A director who can cook is a rarity in food television and without her understanding of our passion it would not be transmitted to you. We are also lucky in our food stylist Ginny Alcock who works tirelessly and unstintingly to ensure the produce we cook for you looks as good as it tastes. No half measures for her.

We hope that over the years a bit of our obsession has rubbed off on you, that you take the choice to travel that bit further to a good butcher or fishmonger, that you look for the best local sources of supply. If you will keep the faith then our obsessions have not been shared in vain. Always remember that food is to be loved, laughed over and, above all, enjoyed in the company of your friends.

Clarissa Dickson Wright
Lennoxlove, East Lothian, June 1999

SALT

Salt is really the staff of life – without it we die. The Russians used to have a punishment whereby you could either spend six months down a salt mine or six months on a totally salt-free diet. You might just survive the salt mine, but you would never survive the diet. Roman soldiers were partly paid in salt, and the word salary comes from the name of that wage. And then there are all the biblical allusions to salt. Salt is, indeed, a vital part of life.

Salt is a great means of preserving. In the days before refrigeration, meat and vegetables were preserved in salt. Anybody who has ever salted anything – a ham or pig's cheek – will know how well it keeps. They will also know the corrosive effect of salt. I have two pig's cheeks that I salted five years ago. I just keep them out of interest, watching them get saltier every year. One of these fine days I'll get round to cooking them.

Whole empires and economies were built on salt. Where I live, just outside Edinburgh, the whole coastline was once a string of salt pans that funded the fortunes and economies of the Stuart kings. Today, though, we take salt so much for granted. It is just something we go out and buy by the packet. I hope that these recipes will give you some insight as to how important salt has always been as a food preservative.

CDW

SPICED SALT

This is the French quatre épices, used in innumerable French recipes. It has a flavour all of its own, and is excellent for adding to all sorts of dishes. Rubbing it into chicken or pork before you cook them is a quick way of improving the flavour of these particular meats. Spiced salt will keep for six months, or possibly longer.

2 tbsp coarse salt
4 cloves
1 blade of mace
10 black peppercorns
¹/₄ tsp ground cinnamon
¹/₄ tsp freshly grated nutmeg
¹/₄ tsp cayenne pepper or
1–2 dried chillies

10 allspice berries
¹/₄ tsp aniseed
1 tsp dried mixed herbs

Pound and grind all the ingredients together thoroughly in a mortar with a pestle.

Store the mixture in a tightly sealed jar in a cool, dark, dry place.

BUCHOS OF BACALHAU

This recipe comes from Portugal, which is famous for its salt cod. The Portuguese 'mother' fishing boats go out every year to the great banks and the Dogger banks and send out the little boats that bring in the cod, which is then salted. There is only one place in Great Britain that is salting cod, and that is in Wales. Salt cod is not easy to find here, but if you ask for it, your delicatessen or fishmonger will get it for you, or even salt it for you.

900g/2lb dried salt cod
450g/1lb dried white haricot beans
3 carrots, chopped
1 small chorizo, sliced
1 onion, chopped
1 tbsp olive oil
2 cloves of garlic
1 bay leaf
1 tsp paprika
2 cloves
Salt and freshly ground pepper

Soak the salt cod under running cold water for 24 hours. Put the beans to soak in water overnight.

Drain the cod and clean it well, then cover with fresh cold water, add the beans and cook for 30 minutes. Add the carrots and chorizo, and cook for another 30 minutes.

Meanwhile, fry the onion gently in the olive oil with the garlic, bay leaf, paprika and whole garlic cloves until soft.

Add the onion mixture to the cod, with salt and pepper to taste. Simmer until the sauce thickens a little. Serve either with potatoes or with rye bread.

SEA TROUT BAKED WHOLE IN SEA SALT

I think it was the Chinese who first cooked a whole fish, or indeed a whole chicken or other type of poultry, in a mountain of sea salt. It looks very impressive, and in the case of fish makes it a lot easier to get it right and not over-cook your fish. It is very important to use coarse sea salt, or it will not form a crust.

1 sea trout, scaled and cleaned
Salt and freshly ground pepper
A large bunch of fresh fennel leaves and stalks
1kg/2¹/₂lb natural coarse sea salt

Season the inside of the sea trout well with salt and pepper, and fill the gut cavity with the fennel leaves and stalks (unchopped). Cover the bottom of a large roasting tin with a layer of salt, 1cm/¹/₂in deep. Place the trout on top of the salt. Pile the rest of the salt over the fish so that it is completely covered by at least 1 cm/¹/₂in all over. Don't worry if the head and tail protrude slightly. Sprinkle a little water over the salt.

Put in a preheated oven at 220°C/425°F/Gas 7 and bake for 40 minutes. To test if the fish is cooked, pierce with a skewer: if it comes out warm the fish will be ready. Peel off the salt crust, and the skin should come with it.

Overleaf: Sea Trout Baked Whole in Sea Salt

SALT YOUR OWN PORK BELLY

This recipe comes from Elizabeth Luard's *European Peasant Cookery*, and makes a delicious salt pork belly that will keep almost indefinitely. It is much easier than going around trying to find salt belly of pork in a shop. You must use belly that has not been frozen, which means that you must buy it from a butcher and not from a supermarket. It is perfect eaten with Lincolnshire Beans, see opposite page.

**Serves a large family again
and again**

1 tbsp peppercorns
1 tbsp juniper berries
A small bunch of dried thyme
4–5 bay leaves
1kg/2¹/₂ lb salt
**25g/1oz saltpetre (see note
below)**
3.6kg/8lb fresh belly of pork

Pound the peppercorns, juniper berries, thyme and bay leaves in a mortar and pestle. Mix these aromatics with the salt and saltpetre.

Dry the meat thoroughly. Rub the spiced salt vigorously but carefully into the skin side, then turn it over and rub salt into the flesh side. Reverse it again and rub more salt into the skin side. Put the meat on a layer of spiced salt in a well-scrubbed and scalded salting tray. Pack the rest of the salt all round the meat and set a well-scalded and scrubbed board with a 1kg/2lb weight on top.

Leave the meat in a cool place, turning it in the salt every 2 days. The weighted board can be removed after 2–3 days. The pork will be ready to use in a week, but it will keep for a long time and become saltier the longer it is kept.

When ready to use the pork, cut off as much as you need. If it is very salty, bring it to the boil in cold water and drain, then put it back into the pan with fresh water. Boil the piece for 1 hour and it will be very tender.

NOTE: If you can't get saltpetre, use 25g/1oz of nutmeg and ginger mixed together.

LINCOLNSHIRE BEANS

This recipe is a variation on the American recipe for Boston Beans. Of course Boston in Lincolnshire was also famous for its baked beans. Since many of the Puritan Founding Fathers were from Lincolnshire, the Americans should perhaps ask themselves whether theirs is a Boston, Massachusetts or Boston, Lincolnshire recipe!

Serves 6-8

700g/1¹/₂ lb dried white beans such as navy or haricot
2 tsp salt
225g/8oz piece of fat salt pork
1 tbsp soft brown sugar
4 tbsp dark molasses or treacle
¹/₂ tsp dry mustard
¹/₂ Worcestershire sauce

Rinse the beans and soak them in cold water overnight or for a minimum of 5 or 6 hours.

Pour the beans into a pan with the water in which they were soaked. Add the salt and simmer, covered for 2-3 hours, or until tender but not broken, adding water as needed in small amounts. When the beans have cooked, drain them and put them into the bean pot.

Pour boiling water over the pork, scrape the rind until it is white. Score into half-inch strips and press on top of the beans, leaving only the rind exposed. Mix the brown sugar, molasses, mustard and Worcestershire sauce together. Add one cup of boiling water to this and pour over the beans. Add more boiling water to cover the beans if necessary.

Cover and bake in a preheated oven at 100º F/200º F/ Gas low for 6-8 hours, adding more water as needed, to keep the beans just covered. Uncover during the last half-hour of cooking to brown the pork and the beans.

PASTA

Now what can I say about pasta? It is strictly Italian, as we know it, as opposed to Chinese noodles, which are made with rice and other ingredients. It has nothing to do with Marco Polo – that's just some nonsense thought up through the years. In fact, pasta dates back to the Romans and the Etruscans, and has been going strong ever since. Instead of a luxury food enjoyed by the wealthy, it has become the staple diet for every part of Italy, and a very good thing too, as it is both delicious and nutritious. It can be made in a thousand different ways, with a thousand different sauces.

I think of all the so-called peasant foods, like potatoes, rice and beans, pasta has now become the favourite easy food in western civilisation. I would have thought everybody eats some sort of pasta regularly – and how good a properly prepared dish of steaming spaghetti can be when served with care, a beautiful sauce and, of course, freshly grated proper Parmesan, unless you are having a fish pasta. I don't know why the Italians never put cheese on their fish dishes. I feel it might be left over from the Jewish cuisine.

The great thing about all forms of pasta is that they can either be served very simply with just butter, oil and cheese, or with some quite complicated sauces that require time and care but that are ultimately worthwhile. The best thing to do is to get a real Italian cookery book, with many different sauces to practise on. You will find that each region has its own favourites.

You will always find new sauces if you have the luck to go to people's private houses in Italy. I once had a wonderful feast on top of a mountain near Lucca. It was marvellous, some celebration or other, and all the villagers joined in and brought

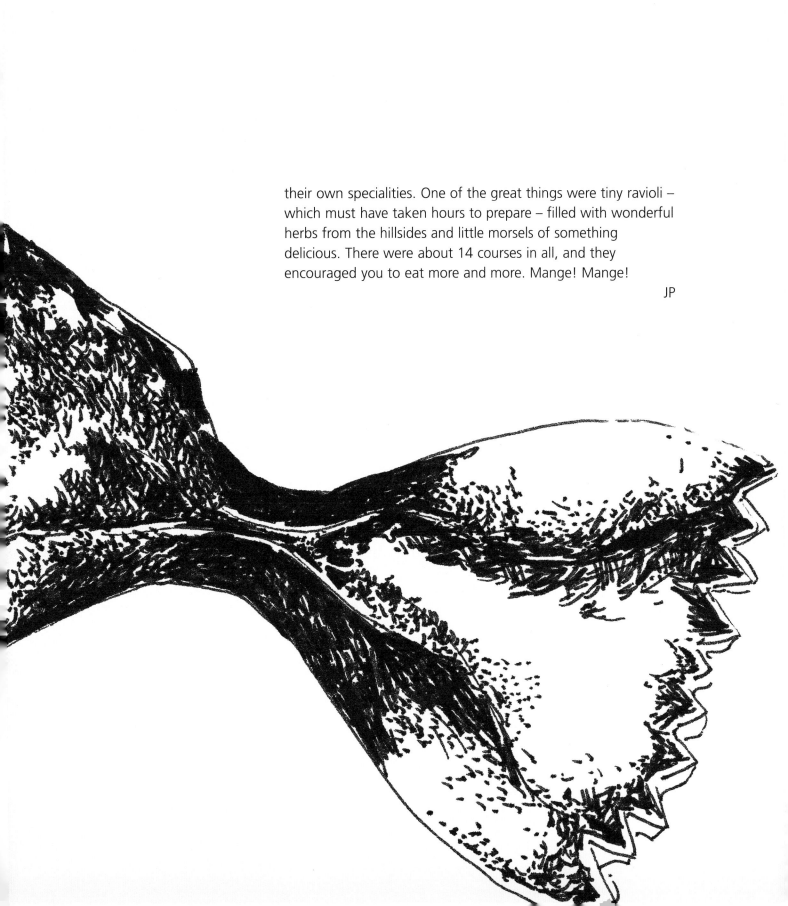

their own specialities. One of the great things were tiny ravioli –
which must have taken hours to prepare – filled with wonderful
herbs from the hillsides and little morsels of something
delicious. There were about 14 courses in all, and they
encouraged you to eat more and more. Mange! Mange!

JP

SPAGHETTI WITH SOURED CREAM

Another pasta dish that is not so commonly found, this is charming to look at and, I think, delicious and very easy.

85g/3oz butter
300ml/¹/₂ pint soured cream
Paprika
Freshly grated nutmeg
175g/6oz Parmesan cheese,
   freshly grated
Salt
700g/1¹/₂lb spaghetti

In a pan large enough to eventually hold all the ingredients, put the butter, soured cream, paprika to taste, a little grated nutmeg, the grated Parmesan and salt to taste. Mix all together while they are still cold.

Cook the spaghetti in a pan of boiling salted water. About 5 minutes before the spaghetti will have reached the point of being very undercooked, put the pan with the sauce ingredients over a moderate heat.

When the spaghetti is cooked, drain in a colander and transfer them to the pan with the butter and cream mixture. Cook over a moderate heat for 5 minutes, stirring gently with two forks. Transfer to a serving dish and send to the table.

FETTUCCINE WITH WALNUTS

This is a rather curious dish, being sweetened with spice and sugar. It is eaten in central Italy on Christmas Eve. I don't know if you fancy the idea of this dish, but it is certainly different and, of course, no cheese is served with it.

Scant 150ml/¹/₄ pint cream
85g/3oz fresh breadcrumbs
4 tbsp granulated sugar
A pinch of ground cinnamon
450g/1lb shelled walnuts
450g/1lb fettuccine

Pour the cream over the breadcrumbs in a bowl, and add the sugar and cinnamon. Chop up the walnuts and add to the bowl, mixing well.

Cook the fettuccine in a big pan of boiling salted water, then drain and put a layer in a heated serving dish. On this spread a layer of the walnut and breadcrumb mixture. Continue in alternate layers until all the fettuccine and walnut mixture are used up.

ORECCHIETTE WITH FLOWERING BROCCOLI – THE SIMPLE VERSION

This version comes from Bari.

**450g/1lb orecchiette
(little ears)**
900g/2lb flowering broccoli
**Salt and freshly ground
pepper**
7 tbsp olive oil
**55–85g/2–3oz Pecorino or
Parmesan cheese, freshly
grated (optional)**

Take the pan in which you intend to cook the pasta, put in the appropriate quantity of water and bring to the boil. Add the broccoli broken up into florets and cook for about 8 minutes. Remove from the water with a perforated spoon and keep hot.

Put the orecchiette into the same water, bringing the water back to the boil. As soon as they are cooked drain them in the usual way and transfer from the colander to a nice deep, heated serving dish. Spoon the hot broccoli over the pasta, and add a little salt and a lot of freshly ground black pepper. Pour the olive oil over the broccoli and pasta and mix very well so that the broccoli florets break up – together with the uncooked oil, which should be the best you can get, this gives this dish its delicious and characteristic flavour. It is good with or without cheese, depending on your preference.

ORECCHIETTE WITH FLOWERING BROCCOLI

This is a famous Sicilian dish, which I learnt to love when we lived there.

700g/1½lb orecchiette (little ears)
85g/3oz Pecorino or Parmesan cheese, freshly grated (optional)
For the sauce:
Salt and freshly ground pepper
900g/2lb flowering broccoli, broken into florets
115g/4oz salted anchovies or 55g/2oz tinned anchovy fillets, drained
900g/2lb fresh tomatoes or 700g/1½lb tinned peeled tomatoes
8 tbsp olive oil
2 cloves of garlic
Small piece of fresh hot red chilli, chopped
¼ onion, very finely chopped
40g/1½oz sultanas or seedless raisins, soaked in tepid water to plump up
40g/1½oz pine kernels

Bring a large saucepan of water to the boil. Add salt, then the broccoli. Cook for about 3 minutes, boiling briskly. Remove the broccoli with a perforated spoon and keep on one side. Keep the pan of water to cook the pasta later.

If using salted anchovies, soak them in cold water for about 20 minutes before using. Chop the anchovies, whether salted or tinned. If you are using fresh tomatoes, put them in boiling water for a minute, then drain and peel them. Whether fresh or tinned tomatoes, remove the seeds and liquid, shake them dry and chop them up.

Put half the oil in a frying pan, add 1 whole clove of garlic and the chopped red chilli, and fry fairly briskly until the garlic turns golden. Take the garlic out. Add the chopped anchovies and tomatoes to the oil in the pan. Season with a little salt, bring to the boil and cook for 15 minutes. If at the end of this time the sauce seems too thin, boil briskly for a few minutes to thicken.

Put the rest of the oil in a second frying pan and add the chopped onion and the second clove of garlic. Cook over moderate heat until the garlic turns golden, then remove it. Add the cooked broccoli, the sultanas or raisins and the pine kernels. Season with a very little salt and a fair amount of black pepper. Cook for about 2 minutes over a medium heat, stirring with 2 forks to avoid breaking the florets. Then add the contents of this pan to the tomato sauce. Mix gently and keep hot.

Back to the saucepan where you boiled the broccoli: bring the water to the boil and add the orecchiette. When the pasta is cooked, drain it well. Place it in a nice heated serving dish, a little at a time in layers interspersed with the sauce. In this way the pasta and the sauce can mix well together with less risk of breaking the broccoli florets. If you are using grated cheese, this too should go in in layers.

LOBSTER

In this country lobster is usually too expensive to do much with other than eat it plain. In fact, it is hard to beat the joys of a plain lobster. When the daffodils are bouncing in the breeze, my fishmonger will have the first lobsters of the season, and I then know that spring has truly come. As the water begins to thaw, the lobsters come up to feed again after their winter hibernation.

There was a time in my life when I cooked on a charter yacht off the East Coast of America. There they have large quantities of lobsters which are available at a reasonable price. Every little seaside village and town has a lobster shack where you can go in and select your lobsters from the large tanks. It is actually a fallacy that the smaller the lobster the sweeter it is. The meat in large lobsters is extremely tender, provided you cook the lobster carefully, and very often you can get a very good bargain on a hoary old denizen of the depths. Although lobster fishing during the breeding season is not encouraged, I recommend that you try to get a lobster with its coral on – the coral is very delicious. It should be taken off and eaten as any caviar, with lemon juice and a bit of bread.

Once, when returning from America via Boston to London, I took advantage of the packages that they do of live lobsters on ice. I brought back six lobsters plus six quarts of steamer clams. I sent these in the hold, and the lobsters no doubt had a lovely time because it was nice and cold, just like the bottom of the sea. When I took them through customs, the official said, 'What is that scrambling around in there? It's alive!'
I said 'It's a lobster.'
He said 'You can't bring those in here alive.'
I said 'Could I bring them through if they were dead?'
He said 'Well, yes.'

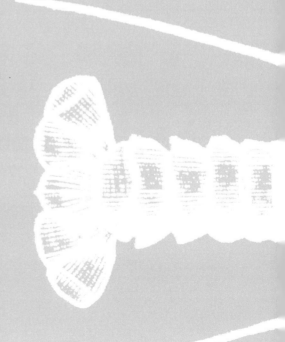

So I started to unpin my brooch, which had a big heavy pin on it.
He said 'What are you going do with that?'
I said 'Well I'm going to kill them.'
And he said 'Not in front of me you're not. Take them away, take them away.' And he waved me through customs.

I took them back to my brother's house, and we had a lovely time cooking them and arguing as to whether they tasted better than British lobsters.

These dishes can, of course, also be done with prawns, or with the cheaper, frozen Canadian lobster, which is finding its way more and more into the shops in this country. You can always tell a Canadian lobster because its head is a different colour red, a more brick red, and it has a triangular shape rather like an old flinthead arrow. If people try to sell these to you as British lobsters, get extremely stroppy with them indeed, because they are not the same thing, and should not be charged at the same price.

CDW

LOBSTER EN CASSEROLE

This dish comes from Sir Harry Luke's splendid book *The Tenth Muse,* which recites his activities as a naval officer. He says he was called upon to lay down his stomach for his country and eat some very peculiar things indeed. This is one of the nicest of them.

1 medium-sized lobster, cooked

115g/4oz button mushrooms, sliced

4 tomatoes, chopped

A glass of brandy

A glass of sherry

120ml/4floz double cream

3 egg yolks

Juice of ½ lemon

Cayenne pepper

Salt and freshly ground pepper

Remove the flesh from the lobster, chop it into chunks and reserve. Use the shell to make a stock.

Put the lobster flesh into a casserole dish with the mushrooms and tomatoes. Stir together half a pint of lobster stock, brandy, sherry, cream, egg yolks and lemon juice, and season with cayenne, salt and pepper. Pour over the lobster and stir to mix.

Cook in a preheated oven at 170°C/325°F/Gas 3 for about 20 minutes. It's a very simple but delicious lobster dish.

LOBSTER NEWBURG

This is a classic dish and one that repays revisiting.

1 small lobster, cooked

A wineglass of sherry

210ml/7½fl oz double cream

2 egg yolks

Pinch of cayenne pepper

Salt

Remove the meat from the lobster. Cut the tail meat into slices slantwise and place in a well-buttered fireproof dish with the claw meat on top. Sprinkle with a little of the sherry. Cover the dish and put into a preheated oven at 170°C/325°F/Gas 3 to heat.

Meanwhile, put the cream, remaining sherry, egg yolks, cayenne and salt to taste in a bowl set over a pan of boiling water, and whisk until creamy. Pour this sauce over the lobster and serve with rice.

Opposite: Lobster Newburg

LOBSTER IN COCONUT

I spent some time in the Caribbean where there was a plentiful supply of crayfish, some as big as 30 pounds in weight, and inexpensive. There was also a plentiful supply of coconuts. As I love coconut, I tried putting the two together, which was very successful. It works just as well with lobster.

2 tsp coconut oil
1 large onion, finely sliced
1 tsp ground turmeric
2 medium-sized lobsters,
  cooked and the meat
  removed
175ml/6fl oz coconut cream
  (see note)

Heat the oil in a saucepan, add the onion and turmeric, and fry over a medium heat for 1 minute. Add the chopped up lobster meat and the coconut cream, and simmer gently for 8–10 minutes without allowing the mixture to boil. At the end of this time the sauce should be thickened.

Serve in heated bowls with a separate dish of rice.

NOTE: To make coconut cream, remove the meat from a coconut, grate it and pour over boiling water. Leave to stand for 20 minutes, then strain through a fine sieve. Or, buy tinned coconut milk (shake well before measuring).

LOBSTER PUFFS MAINE-STYLE

This is an excellent way of using lobster, which I learned from the locals when I was living on the East Coast of the US. If you don't use lobster meat, you can just as easily use crayfish or prawns.

450g/1lb strong white bread flour
1 tbsp baking powder
1/3 tsp salt
Good pinch of freshly grated
  nutmeg
Generous pinch of dried thyme
1 large egg
240ml/8fl oz milk
225g/8oz freshly cooked lobster
  meat, cut into small pieces
Oil for deep frying

Sift the flour, baking powder, salt, nutmeg and thyme into a mixing bowl. Beat the egg and mix it with the milk, then stir it into the dry ingredients. Beat until a smooth batter is formed. Add the lobster meat. Leave to stand for at least 30 minutes in a cool place.

Heat clean oil to 190°C/375°F. Drop the lobster mixture from a tablespoon into the oil and fry until round and puffed out. Drain the puffs on kitchen paper. Serve at once with a side dish of tartare sauce.

CHARLESTON LOBSTER PIE

My mother had a great passion for the American Deep South, mainly due to the novels of Francis Parkinson-Keyes. Then my sister June married a man from South Carolina. This was a dish we often used to eat at home and which my mother stated firmly was an authentic Charleston Lobster Pie. I cannot guarantee that, but I can vouch for it as a very good dish.

70g/2¹/₂oz butter
1 medium-sized onion,
   chopped
450g/1lb tomatoes, peeled,
   seeded and sliced
4 thin slices of stale bread,
   broken into small pieces
1 medium-sized green
   pepper, seeded and
   chopped
Salt and freshly ground
   pepper
Freshly grated nutmeg
Dried thyme
Ground mace
2 medium-sized lobsters,
   cooked and meat removed
3 hard-boiled eggs, coarsely
   chopped
¹/₂ cup toasted breadcrumbs

Melt 40g/1¹/₂oz of the butter and fry the onion until it just begins to colour. Add the tomatoes, the stale bread and green pepper. Season to taste with salt, pepper, nutmeg, thyme and mace. Mix thoroughly and cook for 3 minutes, stirring constantly. Chop the lobster meat into pieces and add to the pan. Cook gently for 5 minutes longer, stirring constantly.

Add the hard-boiled eggs and turn into a casserole. Sprinkle with the toasted breadcrumbs and dot with the remaining butter. Bake in a preheated oven at 190°C/375°F/Gas 5 for 15 minutes or until well browned. Serve immediately.

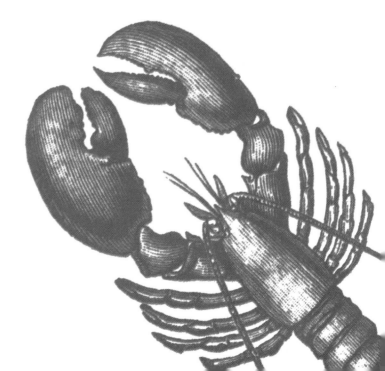

BROAD BEANS

Of all the beans in all the world, I love the broad bean best, particularly when just picked straight from the garden and still tiny, with no need to remove the outer layer of rather grey skin that forms later. I think broad beans are the best vegetable in the world, served simply boiled and anointed with butter and a sprinkling of parsley. Absolute heaven.

Strangely enough you can eat the leaves of the young beans – they have exactly the same taste and make a nice little garnish to add to grills or fish. There are, of course, many ways to use older broad beans, which still have a good flavour, although not the beauty and fragrance of the baby ones. Soup can be made from the pods, using the cooking water for the stock and blending the cooked pods to a purée or putting them through a sieve. The addition of ham stock gives an even better flavour, and a generous amount of cream stirred in at the end makes a particularly fine soup, either hot or cold.

It's interesting to know that the broad bean has been with us since the bronze age or earlier, and is the original for a bean feast. Before Columbus went to America, we in Europe relied on dried broad beans for protein and stodge in the early spring, when other tender roots were just starting. The poor lepers at the Sherborne Leper Hospital, a most humane institution, were always given a ration of broad beans for baking at Quadragesima, the first Sunday in Lent. About a bucketful was their ration, and it kept them going through the Lenten period when stocks of everything else were low.

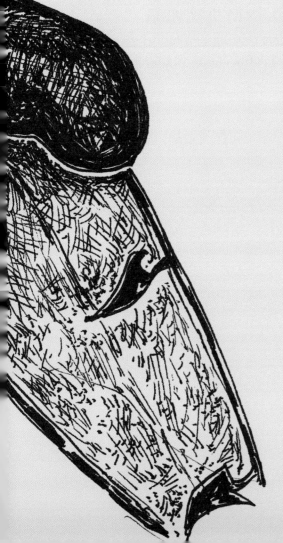

I remember a terrible affair at school when we were trying to sprout dried beans on either flannels or wet cotton wool. One of the girls was fiddling with her bean and got it stuck up her nose. She was too frightened to tell the supervising nun, so the bean stayed in her nose until it started to sprout, at which point she had to be removed rapidly to hospital to have the wretched pulse extricated.

If you freeze your own broad beans when they are young, they are perfectly delicious, but I have yet to find a commercial frozen broad bean that is anywhere near the real thing. So you just have to go out and pick your own.

To skin or not to skin – that is the question! When they are small and young, when even the pods are delicious, the question does not arise, and when they are past their best, which is the only way we can buy them in most shops, the only answer is a purée. It is when they are at that in-between stage that arguments arise. Many chefs insist they must be skinned, and while I agree that this gives you a really delicious vegetable, I cannot imagine that many of us have the time to sit down and skin beans for six to eight people. Of course, if you have an amenable husband and six children then it's another matter.

JP

MINESTRONE

This is a soup to make in late spring or early summer when the first young broad beans and peas appear.

175g/6oz streaky bacon, cubed

3 leeks, white part only, sliced

2 sticks of celery, chopped

2 cloves of garlic, crushed

2 large tomatoes, peeled, seeded and chopped

1 tbsp chopped parsley, plus extra to finish

1 tbsp chopped mixed fresh herbs, such as chives, thyme and basil

Salt and freshly ground pepper

1/2 spring cabbage heart, shredded

115g/4oz shelled broad beans

115g/4oz shelled peas

2.4 litres/4 pints chicken stock

115g/4oz long grain rice or broken up spaghetti

Freshly grated Parmesan cheese to serve

Put the cubed bacon into a large saucepan, place over a moderate heat and cook until the fat runs. Add the leeks, celery and garlic, and cook for a few more minutes before adding the tomatoes, parsley and mixed herbs. Stir the vegetables and season with salt and pepper. (It may be necessary to add a little oil if there is not sufficient bacon fat.) Cook for 5–10 minutes.

Stir in the cabbage, broad beans and peas. Pour over the stock and bring to the boil, then simmer briskly for 10 minutes.

Add the rice or pasta and continue cooking for a further 15 minutes. Stir in extra chopped parsley and herbs, and serve with freshly grated Parmesan cheese.

SPAGHETTI WITH BROAD BEAN SAUCE

This sauce should only be made if you have available very young broad beans with tender skins.

**3 young leeks, white part
  only, finely chopped**
1 small clove of garlic
2 tbsp olive oil
1 oz butter
115g/4oz ham, diced
900g/2lb broad beans
1 small glass of white wine
150ml/¼ pint chicken stock
150ml/¼ pint thick cream
Freshly ground black pepper
**85g/3oz Parmesan cheese,
  freshly grated**
1 tsp chopped fresh savory
400g/14oz spaghetti

Sauté the leeks and garlic in the oil and butter for a few minutes, then add the ham and shelled beans and cook for another minute or two. Add the white wine and bring to a gentle boil. Let the wine evaporate a little, then add the chicken stock and cook over a fairly high heat until the beans are tender. Stir in the cream and pepper to taste, then add the Parmesan and savory. Taste and correct seasoning if necessary. Keep hot.

Cook the spaghetti in plenty of boiling water. Drain and mix with the sauce.

BROAD BEAN HUMMUS

I made this recipe quite by accident. While boiling beans for a purée I thought I would try to make some room in my over-crowded fridge. I came across a jar of tahini paste with only a tablespoon or so of paste left. Feeling a little guilty at throwing it away, I thought I'd add it to the bean purée and make it like hummus.

450g/1lb shelled broad beans
2 cloves of garlic, peeled
2 tbsp olive oil
4 tbsp lemon juice
A good pinch of ground cumin
Tahini
Chopped fresh coriander

Cook the beans with the garlic in boiling water until tender. Drain well, then purée with oil, lemon juice and cumin. Gradually add enough tahini to flavour, but not overpower the beans.

Reheat the purée and put it into a serving dish. Sprinkle the top with chopped fresh coriander.

BROAD BEANS AND BACON

700g/1¹/₂lb shelled broad
   beans
1 tbsp oil
85g/3oz back bacon, diced
25g/1oz butter
1 small onion, finely chopped
1 small clove of garlic,
   crushed
2–3 tbsp double cream
Salt and freshly ground
   pepper
1 tbsp chopped parsley
2 tsp grated lemon zest
1 tsp chopped fresh savory

Cook the beans in boiling water and drain. Whether you decide to remove the skins of the beans will depend on their age and personal choice.

Heat the oil in a frying pan and cook the diced bacon until crisp. Remove with a slotted spoon and drain.

Wipe out the frying pan and return to the heat. Melt the butter over a moderate heat, then add the onion and garlic. Stir and cook until the onion is soft but not brown. Add the beans and bacon to the pan and stir gently to mix with the onion. Cook for about 5 minutes. Add the remaining ingredients. Cook, stirring gently, until piping hot.

BROAD BEAN PURÉE WITH THYME

450g/1lb shelled broad beans
2 shallots, roughly chopped
25g/1oz softened butter
2 tsp fresh thyme leaves
Salt and freshly ground
   pepper
150ml/¹/₄ pint double cream,
   lightly whipped
2 tbsp coarse breadcrumbs,
   fried in butter until brown
   and crisp

Cook the beans and shallots in boiling water until tender. Drain well, then purée with the softened butter, thyme, and salt and pepper to taste. Fold in sufficient cream and reheat very gently to give the desired consistency.

Put the purée into a warmed serving dish and sprinkle over the fried breadcrumbs.

Opposite: Broad Beans and Bacon

BEEF ON THE

The Labour Government banning of beef on the bone in 1998 not only hardened my stance against Mr Blair's so-called Socialist government, but it also made me realise how important beef on the bone was to me. I had always laughingly said that the main feature of my last meal, before I was hanged, would be a wing roast rib of beef. In a world where buying beef on the bone is now rather more difficult than buying heroin – should one want to buy the latter substance – I realise how angry I am at the government's stance and how ridiculous it is. I am convinced that part of the legislation is due to the influence of the supermarkets, who do not hang their meat and would rather not have it kept on the bone because it is difficult for storage.

One of the great features of my childhood was the huge beef wing ribs that my mother would serve up, having perfected the art of cooking them. The secret was to put the joint into a preheated oven at 230°C/450°F/Gas 8 for 20 minutes, then to turn the heat down to 170°C/325°F/Gas 3 and leave the beef there for exactly 17 minutes to each 450g/1lb. This produced a roast that was cooked enough on the outside to satisfy those charlatans who wanted their meat other than very rare. It is a method that I have followed since. A fine joint focuses the meal, and it breaks the ice because people talk to the carver. Men who are able to carve properly are a great asset and are sought after for such dinners.

Clearly I could not give you four recipes for a wing rib of beef, so I have taken other aspects of beef on the bone. When buying a piece of beef, always look for good, clear fat the colour of clotted cream, with a tracery of marbling fat running through the meat. This is the easiest possible joint to cook and will be very self-basting.

BONE

Hopefully, by the time this book is sold, either Mr Blair's government will have fallen or the ban will have been lifted, or both. I live in Scotland where all three of the other parties have said that they will vote to restore this particular joint to our tables. I look forward to them keeping this particular promise.

CDW

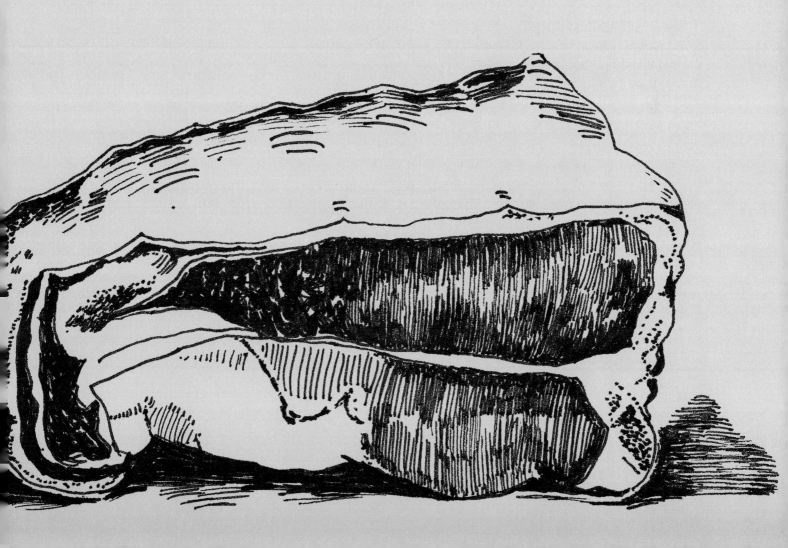

OXTAIL CASSEROLE

This lovely, rich casserole is better made the day before, and it freezes beautifully.

70g/2^1/$_2$oz plain flour
Mustard powder
Cayenne pepper
Salt and freshly ground
    pepper
2 oxtails, cut into pieces
115g/4oz butter
2 carrots, quartered
2 large onions, quartered
A bouquet garni
120ml/4fl oz brandy
3 cloves of garlic
1.5 litres/2^1/$_2$ pints red
    Burgundy
900g/2lb mushrooms, sliced
450g/1lb unsmoked bacon,
    cut into lardons

Season the flour with mustard, cayenne, salt and pepper. Toss the oxtail pieces in the seasoned flour, then sauté them in a large pan in half of the butter with the carrots, onions and bouquet garni until they are a good brown colour. Moisten with the brandy and set it alight. When the flames die, add the garlic and mix well. Pour in the wine, mix again and bring to the boil.

Transfer the casserole to a preheated oven at 170°C/325°F/Gas 3 and cook for 2 hours.

Pour the contents of the casserole into a sieve set in a bowl. When the cooking liquid has strained into the bowl, set it aside to cool. Return the oxtail pieces to the casserole and discard the vegetables in the sieve.

In a sauté pan, gently sauté the mushrooms and bacon in the remaining butter, then add to the casserole with the oxtail.

Skim off any fat that has risen to the surface of the strained cooking liquid, then pour it into a saucepan. Boil to reduce it until it has the consistency of a light-bodied sauce. When the sauce is ready, pour it over the oxtail. Put the casserole on the stove and bring the liquid to the boil. Cover tightly and put into a preheated oven at 180°C/350°F/Gas 4 to finish cooking for 2 hours.

VEAL TAJINE WITH ALMONDS AND ONIONS

A tajine is a Moroccan dish where the list of ingredients used is unvaryingly and mathematically precise, the exact recipe depending on the type of meat or fish used. This recipe using almonds and onions, is a traditional one, although I have added oranges.

900g/2lb veal knuckle, cut into pieces and rinsed
Salt and freshly ground pepper
1/2 tsp ground saffron
150g/5oz butter
1.2kg/2 1/2lb onions, finely sliced
200g/7oz almonds, blanched and peeled
Grated zest and juice of 2 oranges
3–4 tsp finely chopped parsley

Put the veal in a braising vessel and season with salt and pepper. Add most of the saffron, the butter, half the onions, the almonds, orange zest and juice, and enough water just to cover. Cover and cook over a low heat, or in a preheated oven at 170°C/325°F/Gas 3, for 1 1/2 hours, stirring from time to time and adding a little more water if necessary.

When the meat is cooked and almost falling off the bones, remove the veal and keep it warm. Add the remaining onions to the pot together with the parsley, a little salt and the remaining saffron, and shake the vessel so that the ingredients are well mixed. Simmer, uncovered, over a low heat for 15–20 minutes or until the onions are tender but still firm. Correct the seasoning. Return the veal to the pot and reheat gently.

Lift out the veal again and arrange on top of couscous on a hot serving platter. Spoon the onions and almonds on top. Strain the sauce, which should be light-bodied but not too liquid, and pour over the veal.

KNUCKLE OF VEAL WITH GARLIC

A good, rich, comforting dish, this is simple to prepare and relatively cheap to make.

120ml/4fl oz walnut oil
3 knuckles of veal, cut into
    2.5cm/1in pieces
3 large onions, thickly sliced
1 large carrot, thickly sliced
A bouquet garni
120ml/4fl oz dry white wine
550ml/18fl oz veal stock
4 garlic bulbs
Salt and freshly ground
    pepper
6 slices of brown bread
Chopped parsley

Heat the oil in a large braising pot and sauté the veal pieces on both sides until they are a deep golden colour. Remove the meat to a plate. Add the onions to the fat in the braising pot along with the carrot and bouquet garni, and toss them until they are golden brown.

Tilt the pan and spoon off as much fat as you can. Spread the vegetables evenly on the bottom of the pan and return the pieces of meat. Add the wine and boil to reduce over high heat, then add the veal stock and bring slowly to the boil.

While waiting for the liquid to boil, separate the garlic cloves, peel and crush them with the flat side of a knife. Add them to the pot and season with salt and pepper. Cover with foil, turning up the sides of the foil to form an inverted lid to catch the steam and prevent it from diluting the sauce. Then cover with the lid and bake in a preheated oven at 170°C/325°F/Gas 3 for 1–1$\frac{1}{2}$ hours. The meat is done when it pulls away from the bones and is easily pierced by a skewer, which should also come out cleanly.

Measure the cooking liquid. If there is more than 350ml/12fl oz of very thick liquid left, pour it into a pan and reduce it. The sauce will need no other thickening. You can leave the onions and carrots in the sauce or purée them into the sauce and then strain the sauce clear – whichever you prefer.

Toast the slices of bread lightly and put them on a plate. Gather all the smashed garlic cloves in a small dish and serve them so your guests can spread them on the toasted bread. Put the meat on a platter, pour the sauce over it and sprinkle with chopped parsley.

T-BONE STEAKS À LA FLOORS CASTLE

I recently did a demonstration at Floors Castle for the Duchess of Roxburghe, in aid of the Countryside Alliance – a cause dear to my heart – and the Erskine Hospital. The start of the demonstration featured a splendid wing rib of beef provided by the Buccleugh Beef, from the Duke of Clew's tenant herds. It was carried on to the stage by Mr Sutherland of Carffray Mill to rapturous applause. Before I cut the T-bone steak from the joint I said: 'Can anybody tell me that this will do me more harm than a hamburger from meat taken off the bone with a hose pipe.' As I used a pestle and mortar that I'd taken from the kitchens at Lennoxlove, which was the property of the Duke of Hamilton, I suppose this could just as well be called 'T-Bone Steaks Three Dukes'.

55g/2oz butter

1 tbsp olive oil

6 shallots, chopped

2 cloves of garlic, chopped

1 bulb of fennel, fairly coarsely chopped

¹/₂ tin anchovy fillets (about 25g/1oz), drained

2 tsp black cardamom

¹/₂ glass of red wine

4 T-bone steaks

Salt and freshly ground pepper

1 red pepper, peeled, seeded and sliced

Heat the butter and olive oil in a heavy pan, add the shallots and garlic, and sauté lightly. Add the fennel and cook gently until coloured. Add the anchovies and allow them to melt.

Remove the cardamom seeds from the pods and lightly pound the black cardamom in a pestle and mortar, then add to the pan. Cook gently. Strain off any excess fat from the pan, then pour in the red wine. Leave to cook for a few more minutes.

Meanwhile, take the steaks and cook them on a hot griddle until seared on both sides. Season lightly with salt and pepper, then continue cooking until the steaks are done to each guest's specification. Put them on the plates, cover with the sauce and decorate with the sliced red peppers.

CHICKEN

When it comes down to the nitty gritty, and after a lot of heart searching, I think a really well-bred chicken would be my desert island choice. There are so many things you can do with chicken, from the glorious golden roast to the delicious old boiler (always a hen) used for the famous Poule au Pot instigated by Henry IV of France. (His dearest wish was that all his subjects should have the pleasure of eating a chicken every Sunday.) Cold chicken is one of summer's delights, served with a stunning, properly made mayonnaise, or poached in chicken stock, cooled and then coated with a sauce made from the stock, egg yolks, cream and chopped tarragon before being allowed to set in the refrigerator. Real southern-fried chicken with cream gravy is another favourite, simple, crisp, juicy and excellent – 'The Colonel' of those glue-covered bits of tasteless chicken should feel ashamed.

In my youth chicken was a terrific treat, as it should be now. We children were given the drumsticks and, of course, the wishbone to pull, which caused howls of fury from the loser. The grown-ups ate dainty slices of breast which I never fancied, finding it too dry. I still prefer the dark meat to this day. The great prize was the liver, which would be used in a savoury later on. Can you imagine in these days of any amount of livers, only getting one from each chicken? No wonder they were a smart feature at grand dinner parties.

Every country has its own way of preparing chicken, and all of these are easily made nowadays with the wealth of foreign cookbooks and the ability to find the right spices and herbs all over the place. The essential ingredient for all the vast number of dishes is the real thing – a chicken reared in a farm or a backyard and not fed with sinister ingredients in a packed cage. I have had wonderful little chickens from the hills and farms of

Italy and Portugal, all fed on delicious herbs, corn and good earthworms. Simply grilled on wood fires, nothing could be more delicious. And, of course, the French chicken from Bresse, cosseted and properly hung, is a desert islander's dream. So take trouble and choose your bird well.

JP

ROAST CHICKEN WITH HERBED SALT

Herbed salt can be used at will on chops, steaks, guinea fowl and the like. Great stuff.

1 large chicken
3 large cloves of garlic,
**   slightly bashed**
3 sprigs of fresh rosemary
2 sprigs of fresh thyme
For the herbed salt:
4 heaped tbsp coarsely
**   chopped fresh rosemary**
4 heaped tbsp fresh thyme
**   leaves**
2 heaped tbsp fresh
**   marjoram leaves**
12 cloves of garlic, peeled
450g/1lb fine sea salt

To make the herbed salt, chop all the herbs and garlic as finely as possible – use a food processor, a blender or a very good sharp knife. Mix with the salt in a fairly large bowl and let it stand for 24 hours at room temperature in order to dry out.

 Place the herbed salt in an airtight jar and keep it in the pantry, larder or refrigerator to use when required.

 Rub 2 tbsp of the herbed salt into both the inside and outside of the chicken. Put the bashed garlic, rosemary and thyme inside the bird. Do not use any butter, oil or fat.

Place the chicken in a roasting tray and cook in a preheated oven at 200°C/400°F/Gas 6 for about 1½ hours or until well golden and the thigh juices run a clear colour when pierced.

Take the chicken from the oven and let it stand or rest at room temperature for 15 minutes before carving – this makes all the difference. Serve with any delicious vegetables you have to hand, such as tiny new potatoes and buttered carrots.

POULE AU PÔT

This is a wonderful family dish, filling the kitchen with its scent. Evolved from British, French and Italian tastes, it should please every discerning palate.

Serves 8

1.3kg/3lb beef or veal shank
5 litres/9 pints water
1 onion studded with 2 cloves
A large bouquet garni
Salt and freshly ground
    pepper
12 black peppercorns
1 stick of celery
1 large chicken or boiling fowl,
    about 1.8–2.25kg/4–5lb, with
    the liver and heart
700g/1¹/2lb medium carrots
900g/2lb leeks, trimmed and
    halved lengthways
450g/1lb medium turnips
Noodles for 8, about 115g/4oz,
    or 1 small loaf of French
    bread, sliced diagonally
Coarse sea salt to serve
For the stuffing:
55g/2oz fresh breadcrumbs
150ml/¹/4 pint milk
225g/8oz raw gammon,
    chopped
1 clove of garlic, finely
    chopped
4 tbsp chopped parsley
1 egg, beaten
Pinch of freshly grated nutmeg

Put the shank in a large saucepan, add the water and bring slowly to the boil, skimming off any scum. Add the onion, bouquet garni, some salt, the peppercorns and celery, and simmer uncovered for 2 hours, skimming as you go.

Meanwhile, prepare the stuffing. Soak the breadcrumbs in the milk to moisten, then squeeze dry. Mix them with the gammon, garlic and parsley. Chop the chicken liver and heart, and add to the mixture with the beaten egg. Season with pepper and nutmeg (you may not need salt, but taste to see). Beat very well until thoroughly mixed. Stuff the bird and truss it. Add the bird to the pot and continue to simmer uncovered for 1 hour. Add the carrots, leeks and turnips. Taste for seasoning, then continue to simmer for another hour or until everything is tender. Be sure that there is always enough liquid to cover everything.

If you are going to serve the broth as a first course, strain 1.5 litres/2¹/2 pints of the liquid into a separate pan, boil to reduce by one-third, remove as much fat as possible and adjust the seasoning. Either simmer the noodles in it for 5 minutes or serve with the diagonally sliced French bread – toasted in a preheated oven at 180°C/350°F/Gas 4 for 10–15 minutes. (Put the slices in soup bowls and then pour the broth over them.)

Transfer the beef and chicken to a board. Meanwhile, cut the shank into medium thick slices and arrange on a large platter. Untruss and carve the chicken. Pile the stuffing on the platter and arrange the chicken on top. Put the vegetables in pretty array around the meats. Cover and keep hot while you serve the first course.

Serve the meat platter as the main course – it may need some coarse salt to go with it.

A SIMPLE FRICASSEE OF CHICKEN AND BRANDY

It's the brandy that makes all the difference in this nice little dish.

24 baby onions
A 1.3kg/3lb chicken
250ml/9fl oz brandy
55g/2oz unsalted butter
175g/6oz streaky bacon, cut
    into strips
Salt and freshly ground
    pepper

To make peeling the onions easier, dip them in boiling water for 30 seconds or so.

Cut the chicken into 8 pieces (or buy the pieces you wish for). Pour the brandy over them in a shallow dish and leave to marinate for 8–12 hours in the refrigerator, turning them over now and then.

When ready to cook, drain the pieces of chicken, but reserve the brandy. Pat the chicken dry with kitchen towel. Heat the butter in a frying pan and add the bacon and the chicken pieces. Cook over a low heat, turning occasionally, until the meat has stiffened but not browned. Add the onions, the brandy and a little grinding of pepper. Cover and cook over a low heat, again turning the pieces now and then, for 25–30 minutes or until tender.

Adjust the seasoning, then transfer to a hot dish. Serve with some nice little potatoes and a green salad on the side.

CHICKEN JERUSALEM

A 1.8kg/4lb chicken
2 tbsp seasoned flour
115g/4oz unsalted butter
Salt and freshly ground
**   pepper**
Freshly grated nutmeg
450g/1lb mushrooms, sliced
6 tender artichoke bottoms,
**   cut into quarters**
120ml/4fl oz sherry
600ml/1 pint thick cream
Finely chopped parsley

Cut the chicken into serving pieces and roll in the seasoned flour. In a large frying pan melt the butter and brown the chicken on all sides. Season with salt, pepper and nutmeg to taste.

Add the mushrooms and artichoke bottoms. Moisten with the sherry. Cover the pan and simmer the chicken for 25 minutes or until tender.

Meanwhile, heat the cream until just simmering. Pour it over the cooked chicken, stirring to mix well. Sprinkle with the parsley just before serving, with plain rice and peas.

CHILLIES

I come from a family with a long-lasting love for chillies. We always used to reckon that my eldest sister was the milkman's child because she was the only one of us who didn't have a passion for chillies and hot food. One of the earliest memories I have of my mother is of her swallowing teaspoonfuls of Tabasco sauce for fun. My late brother was a great preserver of chillies – he pickled them, dried them, bottled them and put them in salt. When he died I was the inheritor of his chilli collection, which my sister-in-law fondly gave me. It is therefore not surprising that one of my obsessions should be chillies.

Chillies come in all shapes and sizes, types and strengths, from the ravishing little Scotch Bonnet – which if seen growing looks like a field of the prettiest flowers, yet is scorchingly hot enough to take your eyeballs out – through to the nice, mild, gentle smoked flavour of the ancho chilli.

A fascinating thing about chillies is that if you were to take any of the types and put them in a bag in a freezer they will all come out at the heat of the hottest chilli. If you don't believe me, try it and see. The other thing about the chilli is that everyone gets very over-excited about the seeds, when it is actually the ribs that are the hottest part. You have to be very careful when handling chillies not to get the oil in your eyes, or on any other sensitive part of your anatomy – it can be very unpleasant indeed. I remember a friend of mine going to an Indian restaurant and eating a whole small green chilli, and then rushing into the loo to swallow a whole lot of water and wash his hands. Unfortunately he rubbed his eyes as he was coming out and that was the end of a very jolly evening for him.

Drinking water does no good to assuage the heat of chillies. Instead you want to eat a banana, a piece of bread or some grated coconut, or even bite on a lime. However, if none of these remedies is available, should you get chilli on to a sensitive part of your anatomy, then the only thing I can suggest is yoghurt, which actually does quite well.

Jennifer told me a horrible story: in Mexico nurses used to rub chilli oil on to the eyelids of badly behaved children as a punishment. I'm quite certain, having got chillies in my eye before, that the children never misbehaved again.

There are so many different ways of using chillies – it is strange to think how the world existed without them before the New World was discovered. The Mexicans and South Americans treat them quite differently to the Spaniards, Indians or South-east Asians. I have tried to use a range of different methods of cooking with chillis to give some indication of the variety of the vegetable.

CDW

Overleaf: Chiles Rellenos with Cherry Tomato Salsa

CHILES RELLENOS WITH CHERRY TOMATO SALSA

This is a variation on a well-known Tex-Mex dish. I prefer it to the ordinary, everyday Chiles Rellenos. Large ancho chillies, the dried version of poblanos, are sweet and rich in flavour and only mildly hot.

12 ancho chillies
450g/1lb soft goat's cheese
4 tbsp chopped fresh chives
1$\frac{1}{2}$ tsp chopped fresh oregano or $\frac{1}{4}$ tsp dried oregano

For the salsa:
900g/2lb cherry tomatoes (try to find yellow ones to have an all-yellow salsa or mix yellow and red)
1 jalapeño chilli, stemmed and finely chopped
1 tbsp finely chopped shallot
2 tbsp chopped fresh chives
2 tbsp chopped fresh coriander
$\frac{1}{4}$ tsp salt

To make the salsa, remove stalks from the tomatoes, then cut them into quarters if they are small and eighths if they are larger. Place with all the other salsa ingredients in a bowl and mix. You can use this right away or set aside at room temperature for several hours.

Place the chillies in a medium pot, cover with water and bring to the boil. Remove from the heat, push the chillies into the water so that they are all submerged and set aside to soften for 15 minutes.

Lift the chillies out of the pot and reserve the liquid. When the chillies are cool enough to handle, pull off the stalks and scoop out the seeds, keeping the chillies whole.

Place the cheese, chives and oregano in a bowl and mash with a fork to mix. Stuff the chillies with the cheese mixture and pinch closed. Arrange the stuffed chillies in a single layer in a steamer basket. Pour enough of the reserved liquid into the steamer to make a 2cm/$\frac{3}{4}$in layer (make up with water if necessary). Steam for 15 minutes or until the chillies puff out and are tender. Transfer to a platter and surround with the salsa.

CHILLI CRAB

This recipe comes from Sri Owen's *Indonesian Regional Cookery*. For us in Britain it is a slightly unusual way to cook crabs, but I find it delicious, and it totally justifies the work involved.

2 crabs, 450g/1lb each, live or cooked

4 tbsp groundnut oil or other cooking oil

6 shallots or 1 large onion, finely sliced

8 fresh red chillies, seeded and thinly sliced slantwise

2 cloves of garlic, finely sliced

A 2cm/³/₄in piece of fresh root ginger, peeled, thinly sliced and cut into tiny shreds

1 tsp ground coriander

3 tbsp water

2 tsp light soy sauce

1 tbsp lime juice

Salt

Rinse live crabs well before plunging them into boiling water and leaving them to simmer for 18–20 minutes. If you are using crabs that are already cooked but still unopened, plunge them into boiling water and simmer for only 5 minutes. Take them out of the water and leave to cool on a tray.

In a wok or heavy pan, heat the oil and stir-fry the shallots or onion for 3 minutes. Transfer the shallots or onion to a plate, and discard half the cooking oil. Heat the oil remaining in the wok and add the chillies, garlic and ginger. Stir-fry for 1 minute, then add the coriander, water and soy sauce. Stir and leave to simmer for about 2 minutes. Adjust the seasoning and remove from the heat. Return the shallots or onion to the wok and set aside.

When the crabs are cool enough to handle, pull off the hood (which is actually the underside of the crab) and discard it. Cut off the claws. Break the shell open and remove the meat to a plate, separating the white and brown meat. Take out and discard the dead men's fingers in the inedible parts of the body of the crab. I mix the brown meat in with the white meat for this dish, but you can keep it aside and use it for something else, if you prefer.

Cut the shell into 4 pieces and put these together with the larger fragments of the claw shell into a large bowl. Wash them in warm water and dry with kitchen paper. Put them on a baking tray in a preheated oven at 110°C/230°F/Gas 7 to warm until ready to serve.

Heat the wok or frying pan again and stir-fry the chilli and shallot mixture for 1 minute. Add the crab meat and continue stir-frying for 2 minutes or until the crab meat is hot. Add the lime juice and stir again.

Spread the warmed pieces of shell on a serving platter and fill with the chillied crab meat. Serve straightaway.

POSOLE

This is a very good, hearty stew from Mexico. To be correct you should use two different types of dried chillies – the guajillo and the arbol, which is similar to the hot cayenne chilli – freshly ground for the seasoning mix, rather than a chilli powder that contains other spices. The stew is made the day before you eat it.

Serves 10

450g/1lb boneless lamb
   shoulder or leg, all visible
   fat removed, cut into
   2.5cm/1in cubes
450g/1lb boneless pork
   shoulder, fat removed, cut
   into 2.5cm/1in cubes
2 thick slices of streaky
   bacon, diced
2 large onions, chopped
450g/1lb green peppers
   chopped
1 tsp saffron threads
450g/1lb spicy sausages, such
   as Polish kielbasa or even
   the Italian pissano sausage,
   cut into 2.5cm/1in pieces
300g/10oz mild chorizo, cut
   into 2.5cm/1in pieces
20 mild fresh chillies,
   coarsely chopped
1.2 litres/2 pints chicken stock
2 cloves of garlic, finely chopped
900g/2lb tinned white
   hominy (2 tins), drained
3 tbsp chopped fresh coriander
A handful of whole fresh
   coriander leaves

For the seasoning mix:
2 tsp salt
2 tsp chilli powder
1 tsp powdered garlic
1 tsp onion powder
1 tsp ground cumin

$1\frac{1}{2}$ tsp dried oregano
1 tsp dried thyme
$\frac{1}{4}$ tsp dried coriander
1 tsp freshly ground pepper

Put the ingredients for the seasoning mix in a small bowl. Put the cubed lamb and pork into another bowl and sprinkle 4 tsp of the seasoning mix over the meat. Work in with your hands, then set aside.

Fry the bacon in a large covered pot over a high heat until lightly browned, about 6 minutes. Drain off all but 3 tbsp of the bacon fat, then add half the onions, half the green peppers and the saffron to the pot. Cover again and cook, stirring occasionally, for 4–6 minutes or until the vegetables begin to brown. Stir in 1 tbsp of the seasoning mix, and scrape the bottom of the pan with a metal spatula to mix in all the sediments.

Push the vegetables and bacon to one side of the pot, and add all the sausages to the cleared space. Cook, uncovered and stirring occasionally, until the sausage pieces are browned on all sides. Remove the sausages with a slotted spoon and drain on kitchen paper.

Add the cubed pork and lamb to the pot, cover and cook, stirring occasionally, until the meat is browned. Stir the chopped chillies into the vegetables and cook for a further 3–4 minutes, stirring occasionally. Mix the meat into the vegetables, then add the rest of the seasoning mix and the chicken stock. Mix thoroughly, scraping the bottom of the pan where necessary to clean. Cover, bring to the boil and simmer for 10 minutes.

Stir in the garlic and the rest of the onions and green peppers, and simmer, stirring occasionally, for about 15 minutes. Add the hominy and the reserved sausages. Cover, turn up the heat and bring to the boil. Reduce the heat and simmer, stirring occasionally, for 45 minutes to 1 hour.

Add the chopped coriander, cover again and continue cooking until the meat is very tender – about 30–45 minutes longer. Stir in the whole coriander leaves, cover and cook for 2 more minutes. Remove from the heat and leave to cool, then refrigerate overnight.

The next day, skim the fat from the top of the stew, then reheat slowly on a low heat. Serve in bowls, with bread.

CHILLI FRY

This is a recipe for an Indian dish that I found in an old book called *Veraswammy's Cookbook*. Veraswammy was a chef who opened the well-known restaurant on Piccadilly. It is, I think, a successful and slightly unusual dish. The combination of the tamarind and the chillies with the lamb or beef gives a good, vigorous flavour.

**1 tbsp ghee, oil or whatever
   fat you are using**
1 medium-sized onion, sliced
**2 cloves of garlic, very finely
   sliced**
1 tsp ground cumin
1 tsp ground turmeric
6–8 slices of fresh root ginger
**2 fresh green chillies, cut
   lengthways into strips**
**2 fresh red chillies, cut
   lengthways into strips**
Salt
1 tbsp tamarind pulp

**900g/2lb lamb or beef, cut
   into convenient-sized
   pieces**

Heat the fat in a heavy pan and cook the onion and garlic for 3–4 minutes. Add all the other ingredients except the tamarind and the meat, and cook over a low heat for 5 minutes or so. Add the meat and stir thoroughly. Cover the pan and cook for 5–10 minutes.

Add a teacupful of water, cover the pan closely again and simmer until the meat is cooked. This will take anything from 40–60 minutes, depending on what sort of meat you are using.

Add the tamarind pulp, stir and serve. This should be a fairly dry dish.

PARSLEY

The British have always been rather sparse with their parsley, using it mainly to scatter thinly on potatoes or fish dishes and, of course, for old-fashioned white parsley sauce. This used to taste like wallpaper glue with a few specks of green dotted about it, and was poured like some terrible poultice over over-cooked chicken, fish and ham. It can, in fact, be a very delicious sauce when made with a well-cooked béchamel, a little dry vermouth and such a quantity of chopped parsley as to make it really green in colour.

I think nowadays people are using a great deal more parsley and also of different varieties, which is always fun. There are three edible varieties of parsley: curly-leaved parsley, Neapolitan or celery-leaved parsley (which is usually called flat-leaf parsley and is much used in Italy and the Mediterranean) and the strange Hamburg or turnip-rooted parsley, the fleshy roots of which are eaten like celery. In cooking, parsley is used in several forms – in sprigs, often mixed with aromatic plants such as thyme and bay leaf for a classic bouquet garni, or fried quickly in butter or deep fat until crisp and then used as a garnish for fried dishes; chopped, in which case it is usually added to the dish at the end of cooking; and *en pluches*, or picked off leaf by leaf, when it is blanched in salted boiling water and then added to a cooked dish. Fresh parsley is also commonly used for garnishing hot and cold dishes. In all cases, parsley should be cut just before cooking or serving.

Parsley is used a great deal in all the regions of Italy, but seldom raw, sprinkled over something or added to salads. Instead it is usually cooked in a dish so that the heat can bring out the flavour of the herb. A popular base for many soups and stews – called a soffritto – is parsley and garlic sautéed in olive oil.

Originally a Mediterranean plant, parsley has been used

since ancient times. It has been considered a therapeutic remedy for the sting of scorpions, the bites of dog and the relief of menstrual pains and kidney stones. So, all in all, it is one of the most useful herbs to have around.

JP

Overleaf: Lamb Persille

FRIED PARSLEY

Parsley sprigs
Oil for deep frying

Wash the parsley sprigs and dry well – it is important that the parsley is completely dry before frying.

Drop sprigs into very hot oil and cook for a few seconds until the parsley is crisp but still bright green. Drain on kitchen paper.

MAÎTRE D'HÔTEL BUTTER WITH PARSLEY

85g/3oz butter
1 tbsp chopped parsley
Salt and freshly ground pepper
1 tbsp lemon juice

Mix all the ingredients together until well blended. Chill until ready to use. Good with any grilled or fried meat or fish.

PARSLEY PESTO

450ml/³/4 pint parsley (flat-leaf, if possible), chopped
2 cloves of garlic, crushed
¹/2 tsp salt
Freshly ground pepper
2 tbsp pine kernels or roughly chopped walnuts
55g/2oz Parmesan cheese, freshly grated
Scant 300ml/¹/2 pint olive oil

Crush the chopped parsley, garlic, salt and a generous grinding of pepper in a mortar with a pestle to form a smooth paste. Add the nuts and pound again. Finally, add the cheese. When the mixture is smooth, gradually add the olive oil. The finished sauce should be fairly thick.

This can also be made in a blender. Put all the ingredients, except the cheese, into the container and blend until the mixture is smooth. Pour the sauce into a bowl and mix in the finely grated cheese.

CREAM OF POTATO AND PARSLEY SOUP

85g/3oz parsley
25g/1oz butter
1 tbsp olive oil
1 small onion, roughly chopped
1 large potato, chopped
1 small clove of garlic, crushed
600ml/1 pint good chicken stock
Salt and freshly ground pepper
1 tbsp lemon juice
150ml/¹/₄ pint single cream

Roughly chop and bash all the parsley stalks. Finely chop one-third of the parsley sprigs and reserve for the garnish. Roughly chop the remaining sprigs.

Melt the butter with the oil in a saucepan and add the chopped onion and potato. Stir and cook for a few minutes before adding the garlic and roughly chopped parsley sprigs and stalks. Stir again to make sure the parsley is well coated with the butter and oil, then leave to cook over a low heat for 10–15 minutes, making sure the onions don't brown.

Add the stock and some salt and pepper. Bring to the boil, then simmer for 15–20 minutes or until the potatoes and onions are very tender. Leave the soup to cool, then purée in a blender. Return to the saucepan and add the lemon juice. Reheat the soup and thin with the cream (the exact amount of cream will depend on the thickness of the soup). Adjust the seasoning, if necessary, and stir in the finely chopped parsley.

LAMB PERSILLÉ

1 loin of lamb, about 1.8kg/4lb
Salt and freshly ground pepper
Dijon mustard
5 tbsp fresh white breadcrumbs
3 tbsp finely chopped parsley
2 cloves of garlic, finely chopped

Season the loin of lamb with salt and pepper and put to roast in a preheated oven at 220°C/425°F/Gas 7 for 1 hour 20 minutes, less if you like it pink.

About 15 minutes before the lamb is cooked, remove from the oven and brush the skin with a thin coating of mustard. Mix the breadcrumbs, parsley and garlic together, and press the mixture on to the mustard. Return to the oven to finish cooking, by which time the lamb should have a beautifully crisp and flavoursome crust.

MUSTARD

The kingdom of heaven is like a mustard seed – a tiny seed that grows into a great tree. This, of course, does not mean our yellow English mustard, but refers to the much larger plant produced from the brown mustard of the East.

Mustard has been with us for a long time. Once mustard traders were a powerful and influential group within the French economy, very much on a par with one of the City of London livery guilds. Long before the Industrial Revolution produced a metal grinder strong enough to grind mustard seed into the fine powder we know today, it was hammered in a pestle and mortar. This coarse mustard powder was made into a much more liquid sauce, rather like a thin white sauce with mustard. I've tried cooking this medieval version of mustard sauce and very good it is too.

Today mustard doesn't have the importance it once did economically, but it is indeed a remarkable plant, giving us mustard greens, mustard seed and ground mustard. Mustard has many uses, not only for cooking. A mustard poultice is very comforting when you are really cold and miserable. I soak my feet in a mustard bath when I come home from a cold, wet walk – something that I have plenty of opportunity for when making *Two Fat Ladies*. We recently filmed in the Ardnamurchan peninsula in the north-west Highlands, cooking for lumberjacks. I sat in my sidecar as a force ten gale, laden with hailstones, went over the top of it. Everyone else ran to the van. I was very glad to put my feet into a mustard bath when I hobbled home.

Anyway, here we are using mustard for cooking, and I hope you enjoy the recipes I've given.

CDW

PHEASANT WITH MOSTARDA DI CREMONA

The Fascist poet F. Maninetti wrote a cookery book called *The Futurist Cookbook* in which he gives a recipe for pheasant with mostarda di Cremona. His recipe requires that you take your pheasant and bathe it for 1 hour in moscato de Siracusa, a sweet heavy Sicilian wine, and for another hour in milk, and then finish by stuffing it with mostarda di Cremona and candied fruit. I have actually done this recipe and it works very well, but it involves a lot of time, effort and expense. This is an adaptation of his recipe, from Robin Weir and Rosamund Mann's mustard book.

1 brace of pheasants, giblets reserved
5 tbsp mostarda di Cremona plus an extra 1 tbsp the syrup from the jar
115g/4oz unsalted butter, softened, plus a little extra
Salt and freshly ground pepper
4 rashers of back bacon flattened thin
150ml/¹/₄ pint Muscat de Frontignac or any other good sweetish white wine
2 shallots, finely chopped
2–3 strips of lemon peel
A sprig of fresh lemon thyme
1 tbsp plain flour
Lemon juice

Discard any yellowish pieces from the pheasants' livers, then chop them. Chop the fruits of the mostarda quite small. Mix this and the livers into the butter and pat into a sausage shape. Chill this stuffing until firm.

Smear some extra butter underneath the skins of the pheasant breasts, then paint them with the extra syrup from the mostarda.

When the stuffing mixture is firm, cut it in two and put one piece inside each pheasant. Season lightly with salt and pepper, and lard with bacon. Place the pheasants in a roasting tin and pour over the wine. Roast in a preheated oven at 220°C/425°F/Gas 7 for 45 minutes. (They may take longer, depending on their weight – the usual time to allow is 20 minutes for each 450g/1lb, plus 10 minutes extra.) Baste every 10 minutes or so with the wine in the tin.

While the pheasants are cooking, make a stock with the pheasant giblets, the shallots, lemon peel and thyme. Cover these with cold water, bring to the boil and simmer gently. Strain and return to the pan, then set aside.

About 10 minutes before the pheasants have finished cooking, remove the bacon; crumble and reserve it. Froth the birds with the flour and return to the oven to brown the breasts. Once the birds are cooked, transfer to a platter, carve and keep warm in the oven covered with foil.

Pour the cooking juices into the giblet stock and bring to the boil. Add the crumbled bacon, season to taste and squeeze in a little lemon juice to offset the sweetness. Serve the gravy in a very hot sauceboat.

MUSTARD SPINACH

900g/2lb mustard greens
2 turnips, finely chopped
2 sticks of celery, finely chopped
3 tbsp vegetable oil
2 large onions, finely chopped
A piece of fresh root ginger, grated
$^1/_4$ tsp chilli powder, or less
Salt

Wash the greens and shred finely. Shake off excess water, pack into a large saucepan and sprinkle over the turnips and celery. Cook very gently until softened 30–40 minutes stewing should be enough. The greens should produce enough liquid to allow cooking without burning, but check after 10 minutes and add a little water if necessary. Drain and then purée in a blender and return to the pan.

Heat the oil in a frying pan until nearly smoking. Add the onions and ginger, and cook until golden. Stir in the chilli powder, then pour the mixture over the purée. Season with a little salt, stir lightly and serve immediately.

GREEN BEANS WITH MUSTARD

This dish calls for Roman mustard, which is a coarse grained mustard based on Apicius's recipe

Roman mustard:
350g/12oz brown mustard seed
240ml/8fl oz red wine vinegar
350ml/12fl oz unsweetened red grape juice
1 tbsp salt
2 tsp cumin seed, freshly ground
55g/2oz flaked almonds
85g/3oz pine kernels

450g/1lb green beans 2 tbsp mustard oil
$^1/_2$ small fresh green chilli, seeded and finely chopped
1 large clove of garlic, crushed
1 tsp Roman mustard
Salt (preferably Maiden salt)
$^1/_2$ tsp ground mustard seed
$^1/_2$ tsp cumin seed

To make about 900ml/1$^1/_2$ pints of Roman mustard combine the mustard seed, vinegar and grape juice, and mix in the salt and cumin. Leave to soak, covered but not sealed for 36–48 hours. Put into a food processor and whiz for 1–2 minutes or until coarsely ground, then add the almonds and pine kernels and whiz very briefly until they are completely broken up, not over-processed.

Top and tail the beans, then slice them into 2.5cm/1in pieces diagonally. Cook in boiling salted water for 5–10 minutes, depending on their age. They should be tender but still have a slight bite. Drain.

Heat 1 tbsp of the oil in the empty pan. Blend the chilli, garlic and mustard together with a pinch of salt. Add to the pan and stir-fry for 30 seconds. Add the beans and stir thoroughly over a very low heat.

In a small pan heat the remaining oil, add the mustard seed and cumin, and cover. Cook until they start to splutter. Pour over the beans and serve immediately.

STEWED CUCUMBERS WITH MUSTARD

This Georgian dish is a recipe from Hannah Glasse. Ridged cucumbers, which are rather bitter for eating, were really intended to be cooked and respond incredibly well to it. Do not use any other cucumbers for this dish

115g/4oz unsalted butter

3 small onions, finely sliced

3 medium-sized ridged cucumbers, peeled, seeded and cut into 5cm/2in strips

3 tbsp chicken or veal stock

1 blade of mace

Salt and white pepper

1 tsp Dijon mustard

Lemon juice

A handful of chopped fresh chervil or parsley

In a heavy pan melt the butter, add the onions and cook gently for two minutes. Do not allow them to colour. Add the cucumbers and sauté for two minutes, then stir in the stock, mace, some salt and a good grinding of pepper. Cover and stew gently for 6–10 minutes or until the cucumbers are soft but not mushy.

Mix the mustard and lemon juice together and stir into the cucumbers. Allow to bubble for 1–2 minutes until the sauce is slightly thickened. Sprinkle with the chervil or parsley and serve.

MUSTARD DEVILLED CHICKEN

225g/8oz butter

1 tsp mustard

A dash of Tabasco sauce or a pinch of cayenne pepper

1 tbsp Worcestershire sauce

Salt and freshly ground pepper pepper

4 petit poussins, spatchocked and beaten flat

1/2 small loaf of bread, crust removed, broken into small pieces

Take two-thirds of the buter and allow it to soften, then mix in the mustard, Tabasco or cayenne peper, Worcestershire sauce, and some salt and pepper. Rub this mixture thoroughly over the spatchocked poussins. Lay them in a large oven dish and cover with the bread pieces. Dot the remaining buter over the bread pieces.

Roast in a preheated oven at 180°C/350°F/Gas 4 for 40 minutes. If the bread peices start to burn, cover the dish with foil.

Opposite: Mustard Devilled Chicken

OLIVES

There are so many different kinds of olives, it would be difficult
to know which one you really love the best. I keep changing my
mind as I discover different ones in different places. What
wonderful and strange fruit they are. Who would have thought
that those little hard-looking berries could be so transformed
and produce that elixir of life – olive oil.

From the beginning of all Bible tales, olives and their oil,
bread and wine seem to have been the staples, with whatever
else you could get hold of, like a fish or a goat. I remember
when the War came (I was still a child), I had a passion for
green olives stuffed with pimento. I thought they were the best
thing in the world. Of course they disappeared practically
overnight. When all the other children were yearning for an
orange or a banana, I was craving my olives, which I used to
steal at cocktail parties.

Olives are harvested in November and December. Green ones
are picked before they are fully ripe and the black and purple
ones when they are ripe or over ripe. The methods of picking
the olives and producing the oil have hardly changed over the
centuries. But labour has now become much more expensive
and the peasants go to cities for better work, so the price has
risen enormously. However, olives are still affordable. The great
stands of different olives which have sprung up in our markets
– if you are lucky enough to have one – are a joy to behold and
give you a variety of choice. So there is no excuse for buying
those bottled ones with a nasty, watery flavour, which are a
terrible surprise when offered at badly organised festivities.

There is a wonderful traditional Sicilian receipt for stuffed
olives in which the stuffing is a mixture of anchovy fillets and
capers. Also from Sicily comes an Insalata di Olive Schiacciate in
which black olives are pitted, squashed, dressed with olive oil,

garlic, vinegar, chilli and oregano, and sometimes mixed with a Batavia salad. Olive dishes like these with an aroma of such sumptuous proportions, served with wonderful gnarled tomatoes smelling of sunshine, bring tears to my eyes in remembrance of what things should really taste like.

JP

BLACK OLIVE BREAD

Makes 2 loaves

3¹/₂ **tbsp olive oil**
1 large onion, chopped
350g/12oz strong white bread
flour
115g/4oz wholemeal flour
1/4 tsp salt
1 sachet fast-action yeast
(7g/¹/₄oz)
300ml/¹/₂ pint tepid water
(approx)
115g/4oz black olives, pitted
and chopped

Heat 2 tbsp of the olive oil in a frying pan over medium heat and fry the onion until soft but not brown.

Put the flours into a large bowl and add the salt and yeast. Make a well in the centre and add most of the water and the remaining olive oil. Mix to a soft but not sticky dough, adding more water if necessary. Knead until the dough is smooth, then punch it out into a large flat square. Spread the fried onion and olives evenly on the dough, then fold up and knead again for a minute or two to make sure the onions and olives are evenly spread through the dough.

Divide the dough in half and shape each piece into a small round loaf. Place the loaves on an oiled baking sheet, cover and leave to prove in a warm place until risen to almost double in size, about 30 minutes.

Bake in a preheated oven at 220°C/425°F/Gas 7 for 15 minutes, then lower the heat to 190°C/375°F/Gas 5 and bake for another 10–15 minutes or until the bread is well risen and golden. When cooked the bread should sound hollow when tapped on the base.

TUNA STEAKS WITH TOMATO AND OLIVE SAUCE

3 tbsp olive oil
1 medium onion, chopped
2 cloves of garlic, crushed
400g/14oz tinned tomatoes
**1 stick of celery, very finely
    chopped**
A pinch of sugar
**Salt and freshly ground
    pepper**
4 tuna steaks
1 tbsp capers, drained
**10 green olives, pitted and
    slivered**
1 tbsp chopped parsley

Heat 2 tbsp of the olive oil in a saucepan, add the onion and garlic, and cook over medium heat until the onion is soft. Add the tomatoes with their juice, celery, sugar and pepper to taste, and stir together to break up the tomatoes. Simmer this tomato sauce for 15 minutes.

While the sauce is cooking, heat the remaining oil in a frying pan and fry the tuna steaks for 4–5 minutes on either side until lightly browned. Place the steaks in a lightly oiled ovenproof dish.

Add the capers, olives and parsley to the sauce, stir and pour over the fish. Bake in a preheated oven at 190°C/375°F/Gas 5 for 15–20 minutes or until the fish is cooked.

RICE WITH PEAS AND OLIVES

¹/₂ tsp saffron threads
600ml/1 pint hot chicken
stock
2 tbsp olive oil
115g/4oz lean bacon, diced
55g/2oz butter
1 onion, finely chopped
340g/12oz Italian risotto rice
350ml/12fl oz dry white wine
175g/6oz shelled fresh peas
or thawed frozen peas
10 black olives, pitted and
sliced
Salt and freshly ground
pepper

Crush the saffron threads in your fingers and put to steep in a coffee cup of the hot stock while you carry on with the recipe.

Heat the olive oil in a saucepan and fry the diced bacon until crisp. Remove from the pan with a perforated spoon and reserve. Add the butter to the pan and then the onion. Fry over medium heat until softened but not browned. Add the rice and stir until each grain is well coated with the butter.

Add the wine and simmer until it is almost all absorbed by the rice. Add about one-third of the stock. When this has been absorbed, add another one-third of the stock plus the peas if using fresh ones. Stir the rice occasionally with a fork to prevent sticking. Add the strained saffron liquid, the olives, thawed frozen peas, fried bacon and salt and pepper to taste with the final third of the stock. Cook until the rice is tender – it should still be moist but not sticky. It is difficult to give the exact amount of liquid; a little more may be needed or a little less.

ORANGE AND BLACK OLIVE SALAD

6 small oranges
1 bunch of watercress,
washed and picked over
8–10 pitted black olives
1 small red onion, cut into
very thin rings
1 tbsp chopped parsley
Celery leaves, if available
5 tbsp olive oil
1¹/₂ tbsp wine vinegar
Salt and freshly ground
pepper

Cut very thin julienne strips of zest from 1 orange and blanch in boiling water for a few minutes. Drain and reserve. Peel all the oranges, removing all the pith. With a sharp knife, cut down between the segments and remove them whole, free of membrane or pips.

Cover an attractive plate with the watercress, reserving a handful of leaves for garnish. Pile the black olives in the centre of the plate and arrange the orange segments around. Scatter the onion rings, julienne strips of orange zest, parsley and celery leaves (if using) over the top.

Combine the olive oil, wine vinegar and a seasoning of salt and pepper, and whisk all together. When ready to serve, spoon this dressing over the salad.

SNAILS

All over Europe snails are eaten as a matter of course, as they have been from time immemorial. In the West Country and the Cotswolds they are known as 'wall fish'.

I first tried catching and cleaning snails myself when I was working in Sussex on a pheasant farm. There was a large colony of Roman snails, which had obviously been there since they were imported as a luxury by the Romans. (Such snails are to be found all over the South Downs, South of England and the West of England, in fact anywhere there was a Roman settlement. They can be distinguished from the native British snail by the size of their shell and the swirl design up the shell.) I gathered a large number of them – they come out after rain and are easily collected – and put them on a tray of oatmeal, where I left them for two days to cleanse themselves. This is not usually necessary, but it is a safety precaution because snails may eat plants that are poisonous to man, and a certain amount of poison can be contained in the body and so needs to be purged out. The first time I did this my employer, who was sentimental by nature, let the snails out. So I went and gathered them again, prepared them and cooked them. And, of course, once they were cooked, everybody ate them quite happily.

The most commonplace way to buy snails in this country is in tins. Most of the tinned snails come from Turkey, unless you buy the really expensive French ones. Those from Turkey are rather smaller, and benefit well from being cooked in a rather piquant sauce. The larger tinned French snails are useful for Escargots à la Bourguignonne. However, I do urge you to go out and collect your own snails. They are the most frightful garden pest and I'm pushed to see that anybody could feel sentimental about them.

I once had a good friend, Angus Maxwell Macdonald, who started a snail farm in Mull of Kintyre. He was doing extremely well, but was defeated by the distance of his farm from the places he had to transport the snails to.

We are all used to seeing the traditional snail in its shell, served in the special little dishes with a small fork. It's great fun to eat in restaurants and a good ice-breaker. But, in fact, I like snails for themselves and feel that a better use for them is in the dishes where they're taken out of the shell and served with a good juicy sauce, which can be mopped up by bread. I hope that you will try the one I've given here. Once you've got the hang of it, you will not only clear your garden of snails and save your plants, but gain a lot of pleasure out of eating them.

CDW

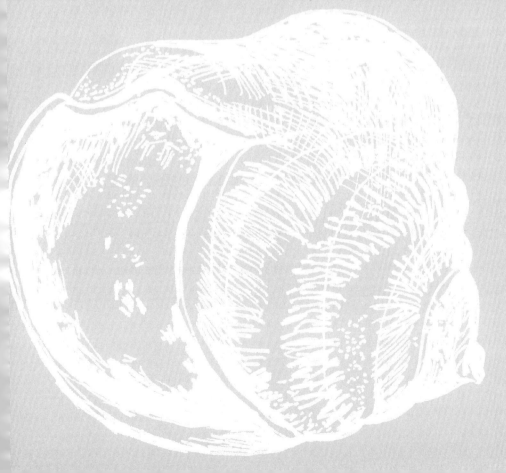

CARRACOLES EN SALSA

This is a recipe from Spain, where they cook a lot of snails. It is unusual because of the addition of the fennel stalks and their fronds, which gives a nice aniseedy taste to the dish, and also the chillies. The sauce is absolutely delicious, and if you don't want to have snails you can use the sauce for almost anything. I do recommend it to you. This is a good party dish, served with plenty of bread and salad.

36–45 large snails, fresh or tinned
Salt
1 tbsp vinegar
4 tbsp olive oil
1 large onion, chopped
3 cloves of garlic, chopped
$^1/_2$ green pepper, peeled, seeded and chopped
450g/1lb tomatoes, chopped
2 tiny fresh fiery-hot chillies, seeded and chopped
Few stalks of fresh fennel with their fronds, chopped
2 bay leaves
A small glass of dry sherry

If using fresh snails, salt them, then wash in several changes of fresh cold water, rubbing them well to scrape off the froth that is their response to the salt. Put them in a deep pot, cover with water and bring gently to the boil. When the froth rises, stir in the vinegar and skim. Lower the heat and simmer gently for 1$^1/_2$ hours. Drain and rinse. Take each snail out of its shell and pinch off the long dark intestine at the end. Return to its shell.

(If your snails are ready prepared, or tinned, start your recipe here.) Put the olive oil to warm in a shallow pan. Add the onion and garlic and sauté lightly. Stir in the green pepper to fry as well. Add the tomatoes and simmer until the pulp melts to make a sauce. Add the chillies, fennel and bay leaves. Add the sherry and stew all together gently for 20–30 minutes or until you have a smooth rich sauce.

Put in the snails and heat them through. Serve the snails very hot in their sauce, accompanied with good country bread and a glass of cold dry sherry. A salad of chopped Cos lettuce is a good accompaniment.

SNAILS IN PUFF PASTRY

This is a very good dish. The anchovies and garlic lend a particularly fine flavour to the snails, and the puff pastry and asparagus give a glamorous gourmet effect. I invented the dish on discovering that all I had in my cupboard when I had people coming was two large tins of escargots. I hope you will try it and enjoy it.

20 snails, fresh or tinned
10 asparagus tips
55g/2oz tinned anchovy
   fillets in olive oil, drained
   and chopped
2 cloves of garlic, finely
   chopped
A wineglass of dry sherry
Freshly ground pepper
About 450g/1lb puff pastry
Beaten egg or milk to glaze

If using fresh snails, prepare them as for Escargots à la Bourguignonne (page 76).

Blanch the asparagus tips, then drain and chop finely. In a bowl mix together the snails, anchovies, garlic, dry sherry and asparagus. Season with a little black pepper and mix well together.

Roll out the puff pastry and cut into 8 equal squares. Place some of the snail mixture on half of the squares and cover with the other squares, pressing down well. Fold over the edges to seal, and glaze with a little beaten egg or milk. Make a small incision in the top to let the steam escape.

Bake in a preheated oven at 220°C/425°F/Gas 7 for 15–20 minutes or until the pastry is golden brown.

NOTE: A smaller version of these makes an excellent hot canapé for cocktail parties.

SNAILS IN THE PORTUGUESE STYLE

The Portuguese eat a lot of snails, and this is a fairly simple recipe. The Portuguese chilli sauce, piri piri, replaces the chilli of the Spanish dish, and oregano and bay leaf give it a particular flavour all of its own. This is another very good party dish to be put in the middle of the table. You remove the snails from the shells rather in the manner that one eats winkles.

2kg/5lb small fresh snails
2 tbsp olive oil
A sprig of fresh oregano
1 bay leaf
2 cloves of garlic
1 onion, cut into quarters
Salt and freshly ground
   pepper
Dash of piri piri sauce

Wash the snails in several changes of water until all the slime has completely disappeared. Place in a large pan and cover with water to come 4cm/1½in above the snails. Add the olive oil, oregano, bay leaf, garlic, onion, some salt and pepper, and the piri piri. Simmer over a low heat for 2–3 hours (the snails should be cooked slowly to make them emerge from the shells). Keep removing any scum that forms on the surface.

Serve hot on small plates with some of the broth used to cook them. Eat with toothpicks or pins.

ESCARGOTS À LA BOURGUIGNONNE

This is perhaps the most famous way of cooking snails. Burgundy is famous for its snails which are raised and nurtured on the vine leaves – the local inhabitants insist that this gives them a particularly delicious flavour. They are certainly very plump and juicy Roman snails. A good strong taste of garlic is vital in the dish, so don't stint on it. It is redolent of rustic French cooking.

The technique for how to cook your snails from scratch and how to get them out of their shells is a basic one, suitable for most snail recipes.

4 dozen fresh snails
Generous 150ml/^{1}/$_4$ pint red wine vinegar
1 tbsp coarse salt
2^1/$_2$ tbsp plain flour
900ml/1^1/$_2$ pints white Burgundy
900ml/1^1/$_2$ pints water
One bouquet garni
2 carrots, sliced
2 onions, sliced
3 shallots, finely chopped
3 cloves of garlic, finely chopped
^{1}/$_2$ tsp black peppercorns
400g/14oz butter, at room temperature
25g/1oz parsley, finely chopped
Salt and freshly ground pepper
Fine breadcrumbs

Wash the snails in several changes of water. Remove the veils that close the openings using a sharp pointed knife. Put the snails in a pan with the vinegar, coarse salt and flour, and let them stand for 2 hours, stirring occasionally.

Wash the snails again and put them in a pot of cold water. Bring to the boil, skimming off any matter that comes to the surface. Simmer for 8 minutes, then drain well.

Bring 750ml/1^1/$_4$ pints of the wine and the water to the boil in a pan and add the bouquet garni, carrots, onions, 1 shallot, 1 clove of garlic and the peppercorns. Add the snails and cook, covered, over a very low heat for 3^1/$_2$ hours.

Make a mixture of the butter, remaining shallots and garlic, the parsley, and a seasoning of salt and pepper, blending it all together very thoroughly.

Drain the snails. Take each one out of the shell and cut off the little black filament at the end of the snail. Wash and dry the shells. Put a little of the butter mixture in each shell, then insert the snail and fill the shell with more of the butter mixture, pressing it down with your thumb. Sprinkle with a few fine breadcrumbs.

Put the prepared snails in a shallow baking dish and sprinkle with the remaining Burgundy. Bake in a preheated oven at 230°C/450°F/Gas 8 for 8 minutes, and serve immediately.

ANCHOVIES

I have a passion for anchovies, as you may have noticed through the years. They are a brilliant little fish, and somewhat magical because they impart their unique flavour in different ways to different forms of food. They have the ability to taste very fishy when you want them to, as when decorating an egg dish, or in a strong anchoiade made with olive oil, garlic, lemon juice or vinegar and crushed, pounded anchovies – quite delicious on a piece of rather burnt toast, accompanied by a little drink as the noonday gun goes off. On the other hand, anchovies can be added to a proper Bolognese sauce (which should have been cooking for hours, until it resembles the texture of jam) and they will give a marvellous flavour without being the slightest bit fishy. And think of Worcestershire sauce, made with secret ingredients as we are told, but certainly containing anchovy, yet we think of it as a sauce for rather hearty meat dishes or breakfast fry-ups.

I have a very good receipt for rabbit, in which chopped anchovies and capers are added at the last moment to give a rather succulent and gamey flavour. Anchovy butter is another treasure taste, spread on meat and kidneys. With the addition of a little rosemary it gives a stunning flavour to any grilling or barbecuing. And, of course, a leg of lamb studded with little pieces of anchovy and garlic is a whole new taste, again not at all fishy.

Fresh anchovies are heaven. We used to have fried fresh anchovies in Sicily. Exquisito with just a squeeze of lemon, enjoyed with a glass of wine on the rocks looking over the wide dark sea.

The anchovy trade goes back to the ancient Greeks and Romans who relied heavily on a sauce called garum that included a lot of anchovy. Anchovy is also one of the main

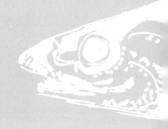

ingredients in Thai fish sauce, which the Thais seem to use with everything, in rather the same way we use salt.

I think it is useful to buy anchovies in nice big jars rather than tins, so you can fish out the required number of fillets instead of having to open a tin when you only want a few anchovies for some reason or other.

JP

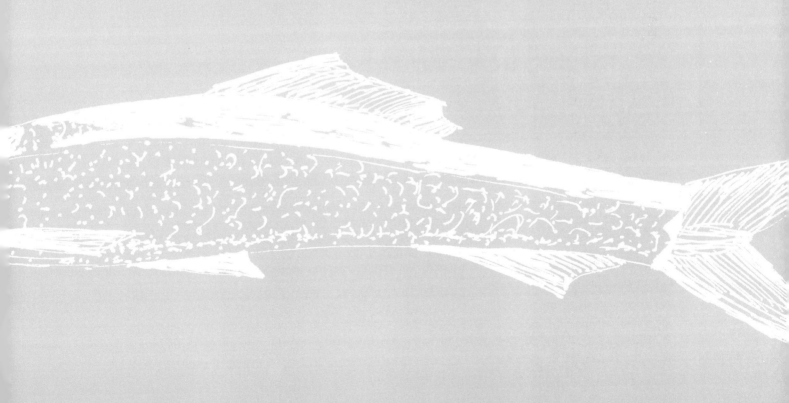

LENTIL SALAD

225g/8oz whole black lentils
4 artichoke bottoms (you can use tinned ones)
6 eggs
Olive oil
Salt and freshly ground pepper
4 spring onions, sliced
55g/2oz tinned anchovy fillets, drained
115g/4oz small black olives
Chopped parsley

Wash the lentils in cold water, checking for grit, then place in a large pan of cold water. Bring to the boil and simmer for about 40 minutes. Add no salt at this stage as it only toughens pulses, although you could add a bouquet garni and a shallot for flavour. The lentils should be tender but not mushy, and depending on their age may take a little more or less time, so keep an eye on them.

Meanwhile, if you are using fresh artichokes, just boil them as usual, then remove the leaves and choke and slice the bottoms into 4 or 6. Hard-boil the eggs, but not too hard – they are better when just a bit moist in the middle. Cut them into quarters.

When the lentils are cooked, drain well and put into a nice shallow earthenware dish for prettiness. Coat the lentils generously with olive oil while they are still warm, and season with a good grinding of black pepper and salt to taste.

Scatter the spring onions over the lentils. Drain the anchovies and arrange over the surface. Place the eggs, artichokes and olives on top in a pretty pattern, and sprinkle with parsley

BRUSCHETTA WITH SAUTÉED CABBAGE AND ANCHOVIES

This is a good cold weather snack.

6 large slices of coarse country bread, about 1cm/^{1}/$_2$in thick
6 tbsp virgin olive oil
3 cloves of garlic, chopped
6 anchovy fillets, drained
300g/10oz white cabbage, very thinly sliced
2 tbsp red wine vinegar
Salt and freshly ground pepper

Preheat the grill, then toast the bread, turning the slices just once, until barely golden.

Meanwhile, heat 3 tbsp of the oil in a large frying pan over a medium heat. Add the garlic and anchovies and sauté for 2 minutes. Add the cabbage, vinegar, and salt and pepper to taste. Cook briefly, stirring, just to barely wilt the cabbage.

Arrange the toasts on individual dishes and cover with the cabbage mixture. Pour over the rest of the oil and serve immediately, piping hot.

ANCHOVY PIZZA FROM NICE

The original pissaladière, the French version of pizza, used bread dough, but I prefer the pastry version as they make it in Nice.

3 tbsp olive oil
900g/2lb onions, sliced
Salt and freshly ground
    pepper
300g/10oz plain flour
175g/6oz unsalted butter
2 tbsp water
15 anchovy fillets
A few black olives

Heat the olive oil in a pan and cook the onions gently for about 15 minutes or until soft but not brown, and then season.

Meanwhile, make shortcrust pastry with the flour, butter, water and a good pinch of salt (or buy it). Grease a 12" flan or tart tin. Roll out the pastry to 5mm/1/4in thick and line the tin. Roll out the pastry trimmings and cut into long strips 1cm/1/2in wide; reserve.

Save 3 or 4 anchovy fillets for decoration and arrange the rest on the bottom of the pastry case. Spread the onions on top of the anchovies. Arrange the strips of pastry in a lattice design on top and push black olives into the onions through the holes in the lattice. Decorate with the reserved anchovy fillets cut into little squares.

Bake in a preheated oven at 200°C/400°F/Gas 6 for 20–25 minutes or until golden brown. Serve warm or cold, either as a first course or in little wedges with drinks.

ANCHOVY AND POTATO FRITTATA

5 tbsp extra virgin olive oil
3 large baking potatoes,
    peeled and sliced
1 onion, sliced
55g/2oz black olives, pitted
55g/2oz capers, drained
6 large eggs
Salt and freshly ground
    pepper
1 tbsp dried oregano
6 anchovy fillets, drained and
    chopped

Heat 4 tbsp of the oil in a 28cm/11in non-stick frying pan over medium heat. Add the potato and onion slices and cook for 15–20 minutes or until almost golden, turning with a wooden spoon. Remove from the heat and let them cool slightly, then stir in the olives and capers.

Beat the eggs in a large bowl with salt and pepper to taste. Add the oregano, anchovies and the cooled potato and onion mixture.

Heat the rest of the oil in the frying pan over a medium heat. Pour the egg mixture into it and cook for about 5 minutes or until almost set. Slide out of the pan on to a large plate, then turn the frittata over, back into the pan, to cook the second side for just a couple of minutes. Transfer to a serving platter and serve warm or cold. This is very good taken on a picnic.

SAUSAGES

A sausage can be the most delicious, juicy and wonderful addition to any meal. It's portable, easy to cook and comes in all shapes, sizes and flavours, utilising all sorts of different meats. A sausage can also be one of the nastiest, most horrible, tasteless and disgusting excrescences on the face of cooking. I know people who do not like proper butcher's sausages, made with real meat, because they have been brought up with the type of sausage that has so little pork in it that it is virtually kosher, with huge additions of bread and grain to make it up.

It has always fascinated me that one of the things the vegetarians most like to copy, in their rather strange habits of making vegetable and grain products look like meat, is the sausage. These, of course, are made out of soya protein, and from what we've been reading about soya protein even the most horrible of cheap meat sausages is probably safer.

There are a number of shops now that specialise in selling nothing but sausages, and very good some of them are. In the *Book of Sausages* by David and Araminta Hipsley-Cox, one was dazzled by the variety of sausages available worldwide. Recipes were given for the larger, smoother German sausage through to the rough-textured French chitterling and the spicy salami-type sausage of the Mediterranean belt where heavy flavourings were once added by way of preservative.

Sausages must be one of the earliest of foods, eaten from time immemorial. One hears horrible stories that the bodies of the Roman slaves crucified on the Via Apia in the Spartacus rebellion were bought by a well-known Roman sausage manufacturer. Or that the Vienna sausages, invented during the siege of Vienna, were never so good after the siege, when human flesh was no longer available.

My first food memory, age 3½ is of a cold sausage and a hard-boiled egg, eaten sitting in the woods by the Royal Horticultural Society gardens at Wisley. Such is the strength of nostalgia that a sausage has never tasted so good. You can very easily make your own sausages if you have the additional equipment to your electric mixer or food processor, and it is still possible to buy proper intestinal skins, although nowadays they're imported.

Since I've become Rector of Aberdeen University, I have 12,000 'children' who frequently ask me for recipes. What can be easier for a student to cook than a sausage dish?

CDW

CHITTERLING SAUSAGES WITH SORREL PURÉE

Chitterling sausage is the French andouille or andouillette, which can be bought in good French butchers or really good-quality stores with a meat counter, such as Harrods or Jenners. This recipe can also be done with ordinary pork sausages. If the sorrel is too strong for you, you can use half sorrel and half spinach. Or, if you cannot acquire any sorrel at all, use spinach and sharpen it with either some lemon juice or a touch of tamarind water.

115g/4oz butter
900g–1.2kg/2–2$\frac{1}{2}$lb sorrel, chopped
Salt
4 andouillettes, sliced into 3 pieces
90ml/3fl oz double cream

Heat 70g/2$\frac{1}{2}$oz of the butter in a pan and add the sorrel and a pinch of salt. Cover and cook over a low heat for 30 minutes or until the sorrel has melted into a purée.

Heat the remaining butter in a frying pan and add the sausage pieces. Fry them, turning frequently, for 5 minutes or until lightly browned. Alternatively, you can grill the sausages.

When the sorrel is cooked, stir in the cream, mixing it thoroughly. Transfer the sorrel to a warm serving dish and place the sausages on top. This is a very good combination and I do recommend it to you.

A SIMPLE SAUSAGE RAGU

On the fourth day of last year's Highland Show, I was running out of things to demonstrate cooking. So I went and acquired some pork sausages from one of the many stalls selling excellent ones – these were quite spicy pork ones with apple, from a prize haggis-maker in Selkirk. I then went to the Scottish Women's Rural stand, where I had been stealing vegetables from the demonstrations throughout the last day of the show, and there tried to 'acquire' a cabbage. However, I was caught in the act and informed that if I wanted any more vegetables I would have to join the Scottish Women's Rural. So I am now a member of that, I'm happy to say.

This is a very good, simple dish, much loved by my students at Aberdeen. I used the brand Isabella's grain mustard relish and apple jelly, but you can, of course, find other less good grained mustard. You can use any sort of sausages you want. The spicy, peasant-style Italian sausages are very good.

1 head of green cabbage or spring greens
55g/2oz butter
1 bunch of spring onions, chopped
8 well-seasoned pork sausages
2 tsp grained mustard
2 tsp apple jelly
A small glass of good ale, the richer the better
1 clove of garlic, chopped

Shred the cabbage and chop across. In a lidded frying pan melt the butter and gently soften the garlic. Add the cabbage and toss until the cabbage begins to soften. Add the spring onions and cook slightly.

Chop the sausages into 5cm/2in pieces and add these to the pan. Stir in the mustard and the apple jelly. When the sausages are slightly cooked, pour on the ale. Cover and cook for 10 minutes. Serve with mashed potatoes.

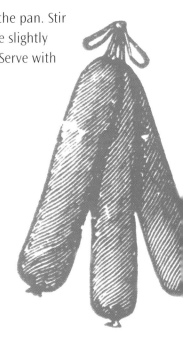

RED BEAN STEW

Since I am always being asked by my students at Aberdeen for easy to make and inexpensive recipes, I am revisiting a lot of those I cooked during my days of drink, debauchery and destitution. This kidney bean and chorizo recipe is one such. You can either use the mild chorizo or, if you like the stronger flavour, use the full-strength one. The colouring of the dish is very good, and the poached eggs look fairly dramatic. In fact, I often think that the finished effect looks rather like a Velázquez painting.

200ml/7fl oz measure of dried kidney beans, soaked overnight
1 onion, chopped
A sprig of parsley, chopped
3 tbsp olive oil
4 tomatoes, peeled, seeded and chopped
$1/2$ tsp paprika
125g/4$^1/2$oz chorizo, cut into thick slices
Salt and freshly ground pepper
4 eggs
150g/5oz home-made bread

Boil the beans in unsalted water for ten minutes, then cook until tender. Do not let them break up.

Meanwhile, fry the onion and parsley in the olive oil. When the onion has softened and started to colour, add the tomatoes and the paprika. Stir and allow to cook a little longer.

Drain the beans, reserving the cooking liquid. Add the beans, the chorizo and a little of the bean cooking liquid to the tomato mixture. Season with salt and pepper. Cook until thickened and the sausage is completely heated through.

Just before serving, poach the eggs in the bean stew. Cut the bread into thin slices and place them in a tureen.

Remove the eggs from the stew and pour the beans on top of the bread, then return the eggs to the stew.

TRUFFLED TONGUE SAUSAGE

This is an ambitious dish and will amaze and delight your friends. The technique of putting a tongue into a sausage casing is just as simple really as applying a condom, though, of course, a lot less fun. Although truffles are expensive, tongue is beautifully cheap and makes this an inexpensive dish to do. People are afraid of cooking tongue themselves, but it is really very easy, and once you have done it you will never look back. The quality of freshly cooked tongue is usually infinitely better than what you get from the butcher.

Serves 6

100g/3¹/₂oz back pork fat, sliced into 4cm/1¹/₂in lardons

4 tbsp spiced salt (page 12)

1 fresh ox tongue, parboiled and skinned

1 truffle, sliced into julienne strips

90cm/3ft fat end sausage casing

1 onion, chopped

1 carrot, diced

2 pig's trotters

900ml/1¹/₂ pints veal stock

Take your tongue, which you have parboiled for 30 minutes in a saucepan of lightly salted water with a bayleaf and peppercorns, then drained and skinned.

Toss the back fat lardons with 1 tbsp of the spiced salt to coat them. Lard the tongue along its length by inserting the back fat lardons and strips of truffle alternately. Stuff the tongue into the sausage casing and tie the casing at both ends. Rub the casing with the rest of the spiced salt, and prick the casing all over thoroughly. Cover with cling film and leave in a cool place for 2–3 days, turning it daily.

Rinse the tongue sausage. Put the onion and carrot into a long, narrow cooking vessel (a fish kettle will do) and lay the tongue sausage on top of the vegetables. Add the trotters and pour in enough stock to cover the sausage. Cover the vessel with a sheet of buttered greaseproof paper and the lid, and simmer over a low heat for 5 hours.

Leave the sausage to cool a little in the liquid before transferring it to a serving dish. Strain the cooking liquid, degrease it and reduce over a high heat until only about 500ml/16fl oz are left. Slice the sausage, pour a little of the sauce over it and serve the rest on the side.

Overleaf: Simple Sausage Ragu

ROES

When the Second World War was announced, the Ministry of
Food put out an edict that it would be a good idea for
everybody to stock up on imperishable food. This was in case
the worst came to the worst, and we found ourselves cowering
behind wet-blanketed doors, having been attacked by the
dreaded mustard gas which did so much harm in the first war.
My mother, who knew nothing about cooking, did her bit and
duly bought a large crate of tinned soft herring roes – no sign
of a baked bean, corned beef or anything else for that matter.
She gave not a thought as to how the roes should or could be
cooked when the dreaded moment came. She just knew they
were one of her favourite after-dinner savouries.

I was brought up in my early years on roe, but the best of all
the roes, the king of roes, caviar. We were living in China at the
time, where they produced lots of caviar from some great river.
We always had it in sandwiches for tea. I have just read
somewhere that caviar is about the best thing for building
bonnie babies, so I have caviar to thank for merciful good
health for years and years. It was considered much better for
you than cod liver oil, which was hard to come by and
disgusting.

On returning to England we were moved on to the red salmon caviar, which in those days was extremely cheap – not any more, I regret to say. I once managed to buy a whole salmon from the fishmonger (very rare) and spent an entire afternoon removing the membrane and then salting it. I love it, especially with soured cream.

Smoked cod's roe is another great treat. Freshly smoked, moist and pink, with brown bread or toast, a squeeze of lemon and a dusting of cayenne, it is a noble feast in itself. Ordinary cod's roe, bought already boiled from the market, can be turned into excellent fish cakes. The grey mullet gives us the correct roe for the true taramasalata.

Lumpfish roe is a very poor substitute for caviar, but looks pretty as a garnish. However, it is the only one that I don't relish. Why is it so gritty? Otherwise the world of roes is varied, delicious and extremely good for you.

JP

HERRING ROES ON TOAST

This is my old standby and one of my favourite savouries. It's not so often seen nowadays. I can't think why. It's very cheap too.

Soft herring roes, about 4 per person
Plain flour
Thin rashers of unsmoked streaky bacon
Hot toast
Gentlemen's Relish or anchovy paste
Butter
Sunflower oil
Cayenne pepper
Salt
Finely chopped parsley
Lemons

Get fine fresh, plump roes. Wash them under hot running water; this will remove the slime and stiffen them up. Drain and pat dry on kitchen towels. Put enough flour in a plastic bag to coat them, then gently shake the roes to coat all over. Remove from the bag, shake off excess flour and lay them on some greaseproof paper.

Grill the bacon until brittle. Have ready some hot toast spread with Gentlemen's Relish or anchovy paste.

Melt the butter with a slug of oil in a good heavy frying pan. When it is just sizzling put in the roes and cook gently until golden brown on both sides. Remove them from the pan with a slotted spoon and drain briefly on some kitchen paper. (If you are dealing with more than one panful, keep the cooked roes warm in a low oven.)

Pile the roes on to the toasts and sprinkle with cayenne pepper and a touch of salt. Crumble the bacon over the top and strew with chopped parsley. Serve with wedges of lemon to squeeze over them.

COD'S ROE SALAD

This is from Elizabeth Luard's *Spanish Travels,* and very good it is too. You can buy cooked cod's roe at the fishmonger or cook it yourself.

Serves 2 as a starter

**1 wing or ¹/2 pair of cooked
   cod's roe**
1 tbsp chopped spring onions
1 tbsp chopped red pepper
1 clove of garlic, chopped
1 tsp chopped parsley
3–4 tbsp olive oil

**1 tbsp sherry vinegar or wine
   vinegar**
**Salt and freshly ground
   pepper**

Skin the cod's roe and dice into 1cm/¹/2in cubes. Mix the rest of the ingredients together and pour over the roe. Turn the pieces gently in the marinade, taking care not to break them up. Leave to marinate in a cool place or in the refrigerator for a few hours or overnight. Serve with plenty of good bread to mop up the juices.

POUTARGUE

As a change from that ghastly marshmallow-pink taramasalata bought in delicatessens, try the French version, which has such a splendid name.

225g/8oz smoked cod's roe
**400g/14oz stale white bread
   (good-quality crumb),
   crusts removed**
300ml/¹/2 pint olive oil
Juice of 4 lemons

Dip the cod's roe into boiling water for a few seconds (this will make it much easier to skin – like a tomato). Remove all the skin, then put the roe into a bowl of cold water to soak for an hour, to get rid of some of the saltiness.

Soak the bread in water for a few moments, then squeeze it dry with your hands. Put the roe and the bread into a blender or food processor and give it a whiz to mix. Then add the oil and lemon juice alternately, a spoonful at a time, blending until you have a thick pale mixture.

If you have no blender, pound the bread and roe in a mortar with a pestle, and beat in the oil and lemon juice – as it was always traditionally done.

SPIV'S SOFT HERRING ROE SOUFFLÉ

No flour is required in this soufflé as the roes produce a good consistency. It always works, and is crisp on the top and gooey in the middle.

Serves 4–5

Butter and freshly grated Parmesan cheese for the dish
450g/1lb soft herring roe
55g/2oz butter
25g/1oz Gruyère cheese, grated
1 tsp salt
Freshly ground black pepper
4 egg yolks
6 egg whites
25g/1oz Parmesan cheese, freshly grated

Generously butter a 17.5cm/7in diameter soufflé dish and sprinkle the sides with a little Parmesan to aid the rising. Place upside down in the freezer until needed.

Remove the black stringy bits from the roes, and run under a hot tap to firm them up. Fry the roes gently in the butter for five minutes. Whiz the roes and butter in a blender or a food processor, but do not purée until smooth. Add the Gruyère, salt and pepper to taste and mix in.

Beat the egg yolks in one bowl, and whisk the egg whites in another until they form peaks. Gently stir the roe mixture into the yolks, then gradually fold in the whites using a metal spoon. Pour into the soufflé dish and sprinkle the Parmesan on top.

Bake the soufflé in a preheated oven at 230°C/450°F/Gas 8 for exactly 17 minutes. Do not peep inside. Eat as a savoury, avoiding wine as its flavour is ruined by roes.

HERRING ROE TARTLETS

Makes about 12 tartlets

175g/6oz shortcrust pastry
225g/8oz soft herring roes
Good dash of lemon juice or white wine
25g/1oz butter, plus a little extra for cooking roes
25g/1oz plain flour
3-4 tbsp single cream
Salt
Cayenne pepper
4oz grated cheese, cheddar is fine
Breadcrumbs, fried in butter until crisp

Line 12 greased tartlet tins with the shortcrust pastry. Prick the pastry with a fork and cook in a moderated oven 180°C/350°F/Gas 4 for 15-20 minutes until very lightly browned. If possible chill the pastry cases before cooking. When the cases are cooked allow them to cool slightly, then remove them from the tin.

Put the roes in a saucepan with just enough lightly salted water to cover them. Add a good dash of lemon juice or white wine, and a knob of butter. Bring the liquid to a simmer and poach the roes very gently for 5 minutes. Drain and reserve liquid.

Melt the one ounce of butter in a saucepan, add flour and mix well. Gradually add 5fl oz/¹/₄ pint of the liquid in which the roes were cooked and stir over a gentle heat until smooth. Add the cream, cayenne pepper and a little salt if necessary, and continue cooking over gentle heat, stirring constantly until the mixture is thick and smooth.

Fold the roes into the mixture and divide between the tartlet cases. Sprinkle a little grated cheese and fried breadcrumbs over each tartlet. Place in a fairly hot oven for 5 minutes to heat through.

GARLIC

I sometimes wonder where we would be without garlic. It is thought to be incredibly good for us as a supporter of the immune system and a cholesterol-reducer. This has long been believed – I think it was Culpeper, writing in the sixteenth century, who said 'Garlic burns away the fat that groweth around the heart'. And it is, more importantly, delicious. I love garlic and feel very bereft when I do not have large quantities of it in my kitchen.

I once had a friend who was determined that the way to health was not to stop drinking the large amounts of whisky that he consumed every day, but to eat a whole bulb of raw garlic every morning accompanied by half a pound of raw liver. This was the most appalling thing to witness. The smell was tremendous, and he obviously suffered enormously from the strength of the garlic. He would then turn to his friends and complain that he found it impossible to get a girlfriend. I'm not advocating the use of garlic in quite this fashion. However, it does add an enormous flavour to so many things.

One of the curious aspects of garlic is that the more you cook it the less strong it becomes, and the more you chop it or work it without cooking it, the stronger it is. A whole bulb of garlic roasted has an extremely mild taste, while a single clove of garlic, raw and finely chopped, is very strong indeed. When cooking it be very careful not to burn it, because that gives it a nasty acrid taste. One way to avoid this, if you're heating it in hot oil, is to remove the garlic once it has flavoured the oil sufficiently.

You can grow your own garlic. It is, in fact, a perfect antidote to greenfly if you grow it amid the rose bushes. The wild garlic that grows so rank in the woods is also extremely good to eat. When I was in Jersey I had a risotto made with wild garlic, and it was very nice indeed. The chef told me that he chopped it up into butter, froze it and kept it throughout the year as the season was so short. One word of warning: do not think that garlic chewed raw conceals the smell of alcohol, as I once did in my drinking days. All it does is produce a particularly nasty and malodorous effect.

The word garlic means 'spearleek' in Anglo-Saxon, which raises the question of what the Saxons did with it. We always associate it with the cuisine of the Mediterranean and France, but quite clearly, if they bothered to name it, the Saxons were eating it, because they didn't name things they had no use for.

CDW

ANCHOVY CROSTINI WITH WATERCRESS MOUSSE

There are no recipes for watercress prior to Victorian industrialisation, because wild watercress carries the danger of liver fluke (a small flea) unless it is picked in running water. At the time of the Industrial Revolution, specially designed watercress beds with a stream of water running through were set up, and quite sizeable areas given over to growing what was the newest food fad of the day.

2 slices of bread per person
Olive oil
115g/4oz tinned anchovy
    fillets (2 tins), drained
3 cloves of garlic
Freshly ground pepper
For the mousse:
100g/3^1/$_2$oz ricotta cheese
1 egg yolk
1 tsp caster sugar
Grated zest and juice of 1
    lemon
200g/7oz watercress leaves,
    finely chopped
^{1}/$_2$ sachet powdered gelatine,
    dissolved in 4 tbsp water
Salt and freshly ground
    pepper
2 egg whites

For the mousse, mix together the ricotta, egg yolk and sugar, beating well. Add the lemon zest and juice and then the finely chopped watercress. Stir in the gelatine and season with salt and pepper. Whisk the egg whites until they are stiff, and fold in. Chill until the mousse is just set.

Brush the bread with olive oil and toast it under a preheated hot grill or in a hot oven until it is golden brown.

Mash together the anchovies and garlic into a fine paste. Season with pepper. Spread this on the hot crostini, and serve with the watercress mousse on top.

PORTUGUESE FISH STEW

For this, use a mixture of fish, choosing from sea bass, sea bream, sole, snook, grey mullet, turbot, red mullet, red grouper, dog fish and sardines. You can replace any of these fish, as long as none of the substitutes have soft flesh. The sardines are indispensable.

Serves 12

4.5kg/10lb mixed fresh fish
Salt
200ml/7fl oz olive oil
6 red onions, thinly sliced
8 cloves of garlic, chopped
Handful of parsley, chopped
**2kg/5lb tomatoes, peeled,
    seeded and cut into small
    pieces**
Dash of vinegar
8 black peppercorns
Dash of piri piri sauce
**2 fresh chillies, seeded and
    chopped**
2 bay leaves
Freshly grated nutmeg
**3 green peppers, seeded and
    cut into strips**
25g/1oz butter
**12 slices of bread, cut
    2.5cm/1in thick**

Trim and clean the fish, and salt lightly. Set aside.

Pour the olive oil into a large flameproof casserole (preferably earthenware, although this is not essential). Heat, then add the onions and brown. Add the garlic, parsley, chillies and bayleaves, then add the tomatoes and vinegar. Stew for a while, stirring occasionally. Do not allow the ingredients to burn and stick. Pour over a little water and add the peppercorns, piri piri sauce and salt and nutmeg to taste. Bring to the boil.

Meanwhile, rinse the fish to remove the excess salt but do not skin or bone. Cut into slices, except the sardines which should be left whole but decapitated. Add the fish to the stew in layers, with the tougher fish at the bottom. Layer the strips of green pepper between each layer of fish. Put the sardines on the top so that they don't break up.

Spread the butter over the bread. Place the bread over the top of the sardines, butter side down. Cover and cook over a low heat, shaking the casserole from time to time to prevent sticking; do not uncover. When the contents begin to boil, and the liquid has soaked and covered the bread completely, the dish is ready to serve. Place a slice of bread and a sardine on each plate and ladle over the rest of the stew.

HEAVENLY RICE WITH SPINACH

55g/2oz pine kernels
350g/12oz long-grain white
rice
70g/2¹/₂oz butter
6 cloves of garlic, finely
chopped
2 medium-sized onions,
finely chopped
900g/2lb fresh spinach,
chopped
¹/₄ tsp salt
¹/₄ tsp freshly ground pepper

175ml/6fl oz chicken stock
55g/2oz Parmesan cheese,
freshly grated

Toast the pine kernels in a dry frying pan over a medium heat, stirring constantly, until golden brown. Set aside.

Cook the rice according to packet instructions. Meanwhile, melt the butter in a large frying pan, add the garlic and onions, and sauté for 5 minutes or until the onions are soft. Add the spinach with the salt and pepper, and sauté until it becomes limp. Add the chicken stock and the cooked rice. Cook, stirring, for 5 minutes or until the rice is steaming hot.

Stir in the Parmesan and pine kernels. Serve warm.

ONIONS STUFFED WITH ROASTED GARLIC

1 bulb of garlic, roasted
4 large white onions
40g/1¹/₂oz butter
2 sticks of celery, finely
chopped
225g/8oz seasoned
breadcrumbs
¹/₂ tsp dried basil
¹/₂ tsp dried parsley
¹/₄ tsp dried thyme
¹/₄ tsp salt
¹/₄ tsp freshly ground pepper
3 tbsp freshly grated
Parmesan cheese
3 tbsp dry sherry

Roast the whole bulb of garlic in a roasting tray in the oven. Separate the garlic cloves, peel and mash in a small bowl to form a paste. Set aside.

Peel the onions and cut off the ends. Place onions in a pot of boiling water and simmer for 20 minutes. Drain and allow to cool for 15 minutes. Then cut the onions in half across the middle and remove the cores, leaving the outer three or four layers of the onion intact. Insert a piece of onion core on the end of each onion half to cover up the hole. Finely chop the remaining onion cores and reserve for the stuffing.

Melt the butter in a heavy pan, add the celery and sauté for 5–7 minutes or until tender. Add the finely chopped onion and the garlic paste and sauté for 5 minutes. Add the breadcrumbs, basil, parsley, thyme, salt, pepper, Parmesan and sherry, and mix thoroughly. Cook on a medium heat for 4 minutes.

Place the hollowed onions in an ovenproof dish. Fill the centres with the stuffing and bake in a preheated oven at 200°C/400°F/Gas 6 for 30 minutes.

Opposite: Heavenly Rice with Spinach

OFFAL

It is quite extraordinary how many people shudder at the thought of offal. In America it is hardly used at all. In fact, when I lived there years ago the butcher would give the lamb's kidneys, sweetbreads and brains to us with no charge, as otherwise they would be thrown away or perhaps given to a cat lover. Most people in England turned against liver in their childhood, having been faced with gruesome bits of shoe leather with some awful dark brown gunge, or terrible casseroles of ox liver cooked to disintegration point and tasting vile, sharp and sour. The same applies to kidneys in various forms. The reason, of course, is that they all were wildly over-cooked. Both liver and kidneys for the most part should be cooked rapidly, and still be pink and juicy inside. Large ox kidneys can be stewed as in steak and kidney puddings or pies, when they are giving their flavour to the gravy.

Brains and sweetbreads are quite a different matter. They need careful preparation as disgusting membrane left on them completely ruins their delicate texture. Again, most people who dislike them have been taste-abused from the nursery upwards. The sweetbreads come from the thymus glands, one in the throat of the animal and one from near the heart, which is larger and rounder. I think they are most delectable, but unfortunately are difficult to find nowadays with everything being banned. You can get Dutch sweetbreads from milk-fed calves at vast expense or the lamb's ones from a good local butcher when the beasts are being slaughtered.

Hearts are excellent when prepared with care. In fact, during the War wily restaurateurs used to serve them carved into strips under the pretence of wild duck.

Chicken livers used to be a great treat as you only got one with each bird. Now, of course, they are plentiful as you are no longer given the giblets with the chicken. Outrageous, I say, and all the fault of consumers who don't demand them.

Tripe is the only offal I have never come to terms with, and I regret it. I like the various methods of cooking it, but in itself I find no flavour. Otherwise I prefer offal to most meats.

JP

ENVELOPED KIDNEYS IN THEIR SUET

This is the simplest method of producing perfect kidneys, if you have a butcher who sells lamb's kidneys still covered in their own suet. They are utterly succulent, tender and juicy.

**3 lamb's kidneys in their suet
per person**

Trim the suet so that it is about 5mm/1/4in all round the kidney. Place the kidneys on a rack in a roasting tin and cook in a preheated oven at 230°C/450°F/Gas 8 (or in the hot oven of an Aga) for about 30 minutes or until the suet is browned on the outside. Test with a sharp-pointed little knife, piercing the kidney: the juices should run pink but not bloody. Place on kitchen paper towels to drain off excess fat.

Serve for breakfast or whenever you fancy, allowing the eaters to dig out their kidneys from the fat, seasoning with salt, freshly ground black pepper and mustard on the side. I rather like them as a supper dish with some plain rice to sop up the juices.

NOTE: If you want to fry or grill kidneys, skin them, slice in half vertically to expose the fat inside and snip it out with some nail scissors. Season the halves and cook gently, making sure that they retain a pinkness inside. Overcooked and curling at the edges, they have the texture of rubber. This applies to calves', lamb's and pig's kidneys. The latter can be soaked in milk for half an hour before cooking, which removes the ammoniac flavour.

STEAK AND KIDNEY PIE

Ox kidney can take far more cooking than other kinds. Its chief duty is to give a good rich flavour, as it does in good old steak and kidney pie or pudding. I really prefer the pie as I find the pudding's suet crust too heavy and soggy, even done by the lightest hand.

You need to have been out on the moors all day to really deserve this pie. So here goes.

225g/8oz rough puff pastry (made or bought)
700g/1¹/₂lb rump steak
225g/8oz ox kidney, skinned, inside fat removed, chopped into chunks
2 tbsp well-seasoned plain flour
1 large onion, sliced
55g/2oz butter
1 tbsp oil
300ml/¹/₂ pint red wine or beef stock, or the two mixed
A bouquet garni of bay leaf, parsley stalks and thyme
Beaten egg wash

If making the pastry, do so first and leave it to rest in the refrigerator. Cut the meat across the grain into 5 x 2.5cm/2 x 1in strips. Put the flour into a plastic bag, and shake the meat and kidney in it until evenly coated.

Fry the onion in the butter and oil until browned, then remove from the frying pan with a slotted spoon on to a plate. Fry the meats in the same pan, browning rapidly on all sides, then transfer to a 1 litre/1¹/₂–2 pint pie dish. Pour the wine and/or stock into the frying pan and bring to the boil, stirring and scraping the pan for any juices. Season to taste and pour over the steak and kidney. Mix in the onion and place the bouquet garni in the centre.

Roll out the pastry until slightly larger than the top of the pie dish. Cut strips from the edge, dampen the rim of the dish and cover with the strips of pastry. Dampen this pastry border, then lay the piece of pastry over the whole dish. Trim the edge with a sharp knife, knock up and flute with a fork's prongs. Decorate at will with any pastry trimmings, and brush all over with the egg wash. Make slits in the pastry to let steam escape.

Place low (third or fourth runner down) in a preheated oven at 240°C/475°F/Gas 9 and bake for 15 minutes. Lower the heat to 190°C/375°F/Gas 5 and place a sheet of wet greaseproof paper over the pastry. Bake for a further 1¹/₄ hours. If necessary, add hot stock to the pie after cooking by pouring the hot stock through the slits in the pie crust.

Remove the greaseproof paper, and serve the pie with buttered carrots, peas and maybe mashed potatoes.

VEAL SWEETBREADS WITH CREAM AND MUSHROOMS

This takes time and care, but is a reward in the end.

Serves 2

2 veal heart sweetbreads, about 450g/1lb
Slices of back pork fat or streaky bacon, thinly cut
2 medium carrots, sliced
4–5 shallots, sliced
Sprigs of parsley
1 small glass of white wine
Veal or chicken stock or water
Salt and freshly ground pepper
2 medium carrots, sliced
55g/2oz mushrooms, fresh or rehydrated dried ceps (porcini)
55g/2oz butter
150ml/¹/₄ pint thick cream

Soak the sweetbreads in cold water for 3 hours, changing the water every now and then, until any blood has drained out. Then put them into a saucepan and cover with fresh cold water. Bring to the boil very gently indeed and allow to boil for 2 minutes, no more. Drain and plunge them into cold water in a bowl under a running tap, leaving them until they are cool and firm to handle.

Remove from the water and trim off the gristly bits, but leave the thin membrane on or they may disintegrate in the cooking. Wrap each sweetbread in a piece of greaseproof paper. Place on a board and set another board on top with a weight to procure an even thickness. Leave under the weighted board for at least 2 hours, or in the refrigerator until you want them.

Discard the paper and wrap each sweetbread in a slice of pork fat or bacon. Secure with thick string or an elastic cooking band. Using an oven dish that will receive the sweetbreads snugly, scatter the carrots and shallots over the bottom with a few parsley sprigs. Put the sweetbreads on top and pour in the white wine. Set the dish over the heat and cook until the wine begins to bubble. Add enough stock or water to cover the contents, and season to taste. Bring to simmering point, then cover and place in a preheated oven at to 180°C/350°F/Gas 4 and cook for about 45 minutes.

Meanwhile, chop the mushrooms, including the stalks, and fry them in half of the butter until the juices run.

Remove the sweetbreads from the oven and untie the string or band. Very gently sauté them in a pan in the remaining butter until they are the palest gold on each side. Add the mushrooms and 2 tbsp of the sweetbread cooking liquid. Pour in the cream, turn up the heat and jiggle the pan until the cream thickens. If necessary, add a little more of the cooking liquid to thin the sauce.

Place the sweetbreads on a warmed serving dish. Give the sauce another twirl, season to taste with salt and pepper, and pour around the sweetbreads. Serve with croutons of French bread fried in butter or, alternatively, place the croutons under the sweetbreads.

NOTES: You can use lamb's sweetbreads for this dish, but it will look more bitty and not so elegant.

After their initial preparations, the sweetbreads can also be simply sliced and fried, or breaded and fried, and then served with many different sauces of your choice. A creamed sorrel purée is another classical accompaniment.

FEGATO ALLA VENEZIANA

All liver is at its best very fresh, tender and young. This dish should be made with the tenderest milk-fed calves' liver you can buy, cut as thin as possible – not more than 5mm/^{1}/4in slices. A good butcher will do it for you or you can do it yourself with a very sharp knife.

700g/1^1/2lb calves' liver, thinly sliced
3 tbsp olive oil
900g/2lb onions, very thinly sliced
Salt and freshly ground pepper

Peel off the skin from around the liver and trim out any nasty-looking tubes, then cut the slices into bite-sized pieces, like scraps of paper.

Heat the olive oil in a large heavy-bottomed frying pan until hot but not smoking. Put in the onions, mixing into the oil, then cover and cook very gently until they are soft and golden yellow, not browning. This will take 30–40 minutes.

Season the onions with a little salt. Turn the heat up and add the liver, spreading the pieces out across the pan. Cook rapidly for 1 minute on each side – that is all it takes. Give a good grinding of black pepper, transfer to a warmed dish and serve immediately with some crisp tomato fritters.

CARDOONS

I owe my fame, my fortune, my being a Fat Lady to the stately, majestic, noble cardoon. Some seven years ago when Patricia Llewellyn, my beloved producer and director, was working as a researcher on Sophie Grigson's *Eat Your Greens* she used to come to the bookshop I was then running, in order to research ideas and to talk about suggested presenters. Somebody said to her that she should ask me about my cardoons. In those days it was my ambition to restore the cardoon to the British culinary scene single-handedly, something that I have to admit that I have singularly failed to do. I had persuaded a friend of mine to grow me a field of cardoons in Lincolnshire, and Pat decided that one of the sequences that should be filmed was me with my cardoons, both growing them and cooking them. It was that that made her think I was quite good at television, and that we should do something together in the future. What the 'together in the future' was, you now, of course, know. I have been more successful at establishing myself as a Fat Lady than as a cardoon-grower, although I'm happy to say that people do still point at me from time to time and say 'Ah, the cardoon lady'.

I still love cardoons, and I would love to see them back on the British table. The recipes that I have given here you can also do with celery, but I hope that you will make the effort to help me in my devotion to the cardoon by going out and demanding them.

An important point when cooking cardoons is to use non-metal pans. If the cardoons touch metal, it makes them turn black. For draining after cooking, use an enamelled colander or a metal strainer lined with a tea towel.

CDW

GRATIN OF CARDOONS

This is a simple and delicious French way of preparing cardoons.

4–6 inner stalks of cardoon
Juice of ¹/₂ lemon
4 tbsp olive oil
12 black olives, pitted and
**   roughly chopped**
1 black truffle, very thinly
**   sliced**
2 tbsp plain flour
300ml/¹/₂ pint white wine
Salt and freshly ground
**   pepper**
4 tbsp Cheddar and Parmesan
**   cheese, grated and mixed**

Trim the cardoons and cut into 5cm/2in lengths. Blanch in boiling water acidulated with the lemon juice for 10 minutes, then drain thoroughly.

In a large pan, heat the olive oil and fry the cardoons gently for 5 minutes. Add the olives and truffle, and stir for 1 minute. Sprinkle the flour over this and stir to mix evenly. Stir in the wine and simmer for 10 minutes, stirring occasionally. Add a little more wine if it threatens to catch. The cardoons should be coated in the sauce.

Season and spoon into a gratin dish. Scatter over the grated cheese and place under a preheated hot grill until brown and bubbling. Serve immediately.

CARDOONS WITH ANCHOVIES

This is the simplest way I know to cook cardoons, but it's very good.

900g/2lb cardoons
225g/8oz tinned anchovy
**   fillets (4 tins), drained**
150ml/¹/₄ pint olive oil
150g/5oz butter
Salt and freshly ground
**   pepper**

Trim the leaves from the cardoon stalks and wipe clean without washing them. Cut the stalks into little sticks, place on a tea towel and set aside.

Put the anchovies and olive oil in a large frying pan and heat until the anchovies blend with the oil. Add the butter cut into small pieces and stir into the mixture until very hot. Add the little sticks of cardoon and cook for 20 minutes without letting them burn, shaking the pan about every 3 minutes to turn the sticks.

Taste for seasoning and serve very hot.

CARDOONS WITH MARROW

This is the traditional French way of preparing cardoons, always eaten at Christmas time. I know you may find it difficult to get bone marrow, but this book is about obsessions and passions, and this recipe is here because I like cardoons with bone marrow. I would suggest that you go out and persevere until you find some. It is worth making the dish. Of course, it's a lot simpler if you happen to have a holiday house on the Continent where they don't have such stupid regulations.

450g/1lb of cardoons
Juice of ¹/₂ lemon
**Salt and freshly ground
    pepper**
175g/6oz butter
300ml/¹/₂ pint stock
**8 tsp plain flour plus a bit
    extra for sprinkling**
55–85g/2–3oz beef marrow

Remove the leaves from the cardoons and cut the white stalks into 10–12.5cm/4–5in pieces. Place in a bowl of cold water acidulated with the lemon juice.

Fill a saucepan with water, salt heavily and bring to the boil. Stir 8 tsp of the flour into a little cold water to blend, then add to the boiling water. Transfer the cardoons to the boiling water and cook until tender, about 15 minutes. Drain and freshen them in cold water, then remove the coarse exterior strings. Wipe the cardoons dry.

Heat the butter in an enamel pan and sauté the cardoons for about 10 minutes. Sprinkle with the remaining flour and cook until they are golden. Add the stock gradually, stirring with a wooden spoon. Continue to cook very gently until the cardoons have absorbed most of the sauce. Season, then transfer to a hot serving platter.

Melt the marrow in a double boiler, or bowl set over a pan of boiling water, and pour this over the cooked cardoons. Serve very hot.

NORTH AFRICAN CARDOONS

Cardoons grow wild all round the anchovy belt of the Mediterranean, and are particularly popular in North Africa. The brilliant African cook, Alaphia Bidwell, once went on a holiday to the Rif mountains and brought me back some wild North African cardoons. They were very prickly, but had an extremely good flavour.

4–6 stalks of cardoon
Juice of ¹/₂ lemon
2 eggs
Flour for coating
Salt and freshly ground
**   pepper**
Olive oil for shallow frying
For the stuffing:
225g/8oz minced lamb
2 cloves of garlic, finely
**   chopped**
1 onion, finely chopped
1 bunch of fresh coriander,
**   chopped**
1 tsp ground cumin

Mix together all the stuffing ingredients in a bowl. Cover and leave in a cool place for 1 hour.

Trim the cardoon stalks and cut into 5cm/2in lengths. Blanch in boiling water acidulated with the lemon juice for 10 minutes. Drain and plunge into cold water, then drain again thoroughly.

Make a sandwich with two pieces of cardoon and the stuffing in the centre. Repeat this process until all the cardoon is used up. Beat the eggs in a shallow dish. Season the flour with salt and pepper and place on a plate.

Heat the olive oil in a wide frying pan over a medium heat. Coat the cardoon sandwiches in flour, then dip into the egg and shallow fry for 15 minutes, turning occasionally, until they are browned. Do this fairly slowly as the heat needs to penetrate through the cardoons to cook the stuffing. Drain and serve immediately.

OYSTERS

Much as I loved *Alice Through the Looking Glass*, I remember feeling terribly sad, if not moved to tears by The Walrus and the Carpenter who eat up all the dear little oysters that were following them with such faith. 'And thick and fast they came at last, and more and more and more. "I weep for you," the Walrus said. "I deeply sympathise." With sobs and tears he sorted out those of the largest size, holding his pocket handkerchief before his streaming eyes. But answer came there none – and this was scarcely odd because they'd eaten every one.'

What a tale for the nursery, but I soon got over it after eating my first oyster with great relish. I have had a passion for them ever since, my favourite being the flat natives, which cannot be bettered anywhere in the world.

I once did a piece for *Food and Drink* in the clear waters of Galway Bay. The water coming down from the Byrne is drained through the rock and is so clean that the oysters don't even have to be rinsed. We spent two freezing hours in an open boat, lifting oysters of such size, taste and succulence to make any walrus weep. I must have had a good four dozen by the end of the day, straight from a chilled sea, really sumptuous, like kissing a mermaid. Neither the cameraman nor the soundman had ever tasted an oyster, and when I made them try one they just puked and spat it out. More fool they. We arrived back at the harbour, frozen stiff, to be met by the charming fish bar girls bearing great tumblers of hot spiced whisky, and then partied on into the night with an Irish band, more oysters, lobsters and crabs. I can't remember better oysters, though of course our own Royal Whitstables and Pyefleets from Colchester are magnificent. I infinitely prefer them to the French belons or armoricaines and the Portuguese or Pacific oysters which are eaten all over France and now here.

Oysters can now be bought all year round, which I think is a mistake – they take on a rather nasty creamy texture during the breeding season which I dislike intensely, although many people seem quite happy with them. I would use them for cooking then. I wouldn't dream of cooking a native, as it would be a terrible crime. All they need is a squeeze of lemon and some freshly ground black pepper, and Guinness, Champagne or Chablis to accompany.

It is quite easy now to buy oysters from a good fishmonger or have them sent from wherever is nearest to you. They pack them in baskets with seaweed and send them by train overnight. John Noble at Loch Fyne in Scotland does a roaring trade. We have them in our local market every week. You can soon learn the art of opening them if shown by an expert, or you can use a lever-operated oyster opener, so don't be put off.

JP

OYSTERS FLORENTINE

There is no doubt that the best way of eating oysters is raw from the shell, but there are many ways to serve cooked oysters for the more squeamish.

Eggs and oysters as required
Salt
Freshly ground black pepper
Spinach

Put a good dollop of spinach leaves, stewed in butter, in the bottoms of scallop shells. Add oysters on top, cover with a Mornay sauce to which the liquor from the oysters has been added, and sprinkle with freshly grated Parmesan. Brown in the oven or under the grill.

OYSTER LOAVES

4 baps, small brioches or small French sticks
150g/5oz unsalted butter, melted
16-20 oysters
8fl oz double cream
Cayenne pepper
Salt
Freshly ground black pepper
Little grated lemon rind
Squeeze of lemon juice

Cut a slice from the top of the chosen roll or brioche and carefully scoop out most of the crumbs. Brush the inside and lids of the cases with melted butter and crisp them in a pre-heated oven (425°F/220°C/Gas 7) for 5-8 minutes, but checking during cooking time to ensure they are not getting too crisp.

Open the oysters, strain their liquid and reserve. Heat the remaining butter in a saucepan, add the oysters and briefly fry in the butter just to stiffen slightly – this should not take more than a minute. Remove oysters and cut in two. Add the oyster liquor to the pan and boil contents for a few minutes to reduce. Add cream, cayenne pepper, salt and black pepper and simmer gently.

Taste, adjust seasoning if necessary then add a little grated lemon rind and a squeeze of lemon juice. Add oysters to sauce and reheat for a few seconds before dividing between the bread cases.

Replace lids and serve.

OYSTERS IN CHAMPAGNE

This is very grand, from the Château de Saran, near Epernay, which belongs to the famous Moët & Chandon.

36 oysters
150ml/¼ pint good fish stock
150ml/¼ pint non-vintage
    Champagne
3 tbsp truffle juice (optional)
150ml/¼ pint double cream or
    crème fraîche
55g/2oz unsalted butter, cut into
    small pieces

Open the oysters, keeping the deep half shells. Put them in a casserole with their liquor and set over a low flame until the liquid whitens. Remove the oysters from the pan with a slotted spoon and keep warm.

Add to the casserole the fish stock, Champagne and truffle juice, then cook to reduce by a third. Stir in the cream and reduce again until you have a rich sauce the colour of ivory. Enrich with the butter, stirred into the sauce little by little.

Place an oyster into each shell, cover with the sauce and serve at once.

OYSTERS ROCKEFELLER

This receipt was invented, so history relates, at Antoine's, the famous New Orleans restaurant.

48 oysters
115g/4oz unsalted butter
8 rashers of streaky bacon,
    crisply fried and crumbled
2 handfuls of spinach, finely
    chopped
3 tbsp finely chopped parsley
3 tbsp finely chopped celery
    leaves
3 tbsp finely chopped spring
    onions
6 tbsp dry breadcrumbs (home-
    made)
½ tsp salt
Tabasco sauce
Pernod or Pastis Ricard

Open the oysters, leaving them with their juices in their deep half shell. Detach them from the shell so they will be easy to eat.

Melt the butter in a saucepan and add the bacon crumbles, spinach, parsley, celery leaves, spring onions, breadcrumbs, salt and Tabasco to taste. Cook the mixture over a low heat for about 5 minutes, stirring the while, until you have a lightly cooked stuffing. Check the seasoning.

Divide the stuffing among the oysters, spooning it on top of them. Place in an oven dish on a bed of coarse salt to keep them steady, then either grill them or bake in a preheated oven at 230°C/450°F/Gas 8 until the oysters are lightly browned and bubbling.

Just before serving, drip a few drops of Pernod on to each oyster. For ease, use an eye dropper.

Opposite: Oysters in Champagne

PHEASANT

Anyone who's acquainted with my life story will know that in 1982, following the death of my dear Clive, I went into a monumental drinking spree which was merely a continuation of my life so far. So bad was it that I didn't notice that the Falklands war was happening. One memorable day I was standing in the rain under an umbrella, watching a parade go by. I asked a young man, 'What is this parade for?' and he said, 'It's the Falklands parade'. I said, 'Did something happen in the Falklands?' and he fled. In an attempt to pull myself together, I obtained – by slightly dubious means – a job cooking on a pheasant farm for a remarkable woman named Rebecca Hardy.

As I've said many times before, it was she who knocked my cooking on from being merely good to being professionally creative. She was the sort of mistress who came home and said, 'Oh good, there are 30 pints of cream in the fridge. What are you going to make?' She reared 25,000 pheasants a year. I helped to collect the eggs and feed the chicks, and did all the everyday running of the farm. At the end of the year the pheasants were shot. Some of them were sold, and the rest were left for me to cook. So, needless to say, I've cooked a great deal of pheasant in my time. I came to understand the story of the small boy, who, arriving at prep school and being asked what he wanted to eat, said: 'Nothing that's any trouble, just a little pheasant.' Or, indeed, to understand my Grandmother's remark: 'But Molly, a doctor is somebody one sends a pheasant to at Christmas.'

It is a great triumph to the pheasant that I continue to enjoy it. I find it a most versatile bird, and one that I've never tired of cooking. Here are a few pheasant recipes for those of you who find that your husband is rather too good a shot and you have a freezer full of pheasants, some of which may not be in the first flush of youth. I wish you luck with them. I'm with you all the way.

CDW

GEORGIAN PHEASANT

Georgian here refers to that part of southern Russia, not to either the period or the American state. This recipe is one of the classic ways of cooking pheasant and is perfectly delicious.

1 pheasant, drawn and trussed (with barding fat)
225g/8oz walnut halves
Juice of 4 oranges (use blood oranges if possible)
900g/2lb seedless white grapes
150ml/¹/₄ pint sweet white wine
150ml/¹/₄ pint China tea
15g/¹/₂oz butter
Salt and freshly ground pepper
300ml/¹/₂ pint reduced game stock

Put the pheasant in a flameproof casserole with the walnuts. Moisten with the orange juice, sweet white wine and tea. Add the butter and season with salt and pepper. Cover the casserole. Bring the liquid to the boil, then reduce the heat and simmer gently for 45 minutes, adding the grapes after 25 minutes.

Remove the pheasant, reserving the cooking liquid and walnuts. Discard the barding fat and untruss the pheasant. Place it in a roasting tin and put it in a preheated oven at 230°C/450°F/Gas 8 for 20 minutes to brown the breast. Then place the pheasant in a serving dish, surround with the walnuts and keep warm.

Pour the cooking liquid into a saucepan and boil to reduce until it is syrupy. Add the reduced game stock. Strain the sauce and pour it over the pheasant.

ALSATIAN PHEASANT

This is a dish from the Alsace region on the French/German border. The recipe calls for a pepperoni sausage, but if you cannot find one, any dry spicy pork sausage will do.

70g/2$\frac{1}{2}$oz butter
450g/1lb sauerkraut, rinsed and drained
225g/8oz unsmoked streaky bacon, cut into 4 pieces
1 pepperoni sausage, about 15cm/6in long, sliced
1 large onion, finely chopped
4 juniper berries
1 bay leaf
500ml/16fl oz dry white wine
Salt and freshly ground pepper
2 pheasants, drawn and trussed

In a 25cm/10in pan or flameproof casserole, place 40g/1$\frac{1}{2}$oz of the butter, the sauerkraut, bacon, sausage, onion, juniper berries, bay leaf, wine, and some salt and pepper. Cover the pan and cook over a low heat for 30 minutes.

In another pan melt the remaining butter over a low heat and brown the pheasants on all sides for about 30 minutes.

Add the pheasants to the first pan, cover and cook gently for a further 30 minutes or until the meat is tender. Remove the trussing string, cut each pheasant in half lengthways and place on a deep serving platter surrounded by the sauerkraut mixture.

PHEASANT WITH FENNEL

In my days as a pheasant farmer, I was interested to see how energetically the pheasants savaged the fennel in my vegetable garden. Game birds are, of course, potty about aniseed and this recipe is my revenge.

1 pheasant, drawn and
    jointed
2–3 tbsp plain flour
55g/2oz butter
A glass of white wine
1 tbsp brandy
300ml/^{1}/$_2$ pint pheasant stock
Salt and freshly ground
    pepper
1 large bulb of fennel, finely
    sliced
1 onion, finely chopped
150ml/^{1}/$_4$ pint double cream
1 tbsp chopped fennel leaf
115g/4oz bacon, chopped
    into lardons and fried
    until crisp

Coat the pheasant pieces in flour, then sauté in the butter in a flameproof casserole. Stir in sufficient flour to absorb the fat, and blend in the wine, brandy, stock, and a seasoning of salt and pepper. Add the sliced fennel and the onion, and bring to simmering point. Cover the casserole and put into a preheated oven at 180°C/350°F/Gas 4 to cook for 45 minutes.

Move the pheasant joints to a warm serving dish. Stir the cream into the sauce and heat through without boiling. Pour over the pheasant. Garnish with the chopped fennel leaf and the lardons.

MIDI PHEASANT

This comes from that excellent book, *The Game Cookery Book* by Julia Drisdell, now sadly out of print.

6 tbsp olive oil

4 medium-sized onions, finely sliced

1 large pheasant, drawn and trussed

6 tomatoes, peeled, seeded and coarsely chopped

1 red pepper, seeded and thickly sliced

1 green pepper, seeded and thickly sliced

6 courgettes, peeled and thickly sliced

2 aubergines, peeled and thickly sliced

1 cucumber, peeled and thickly sliced

Salt and freshly ground pepper

6 cloves of garlic, crushed

90ml/3floz stock or water

Heat the oil and cook the onions over a low heat until they are translucent. Put them into a cooking pot and lay the pheasant, breast down, on top. Place the tomatoes, peppers, courgettes, aubergines and cucumber round the bird. Season with salt and pepper, and add the garlic. Moisten with the stock or water (the vegetables will make their own moisture).

Cover and cook in a preheated oven at 150°C/300°F/Gas 2 for 2 hours. Remove the lid and turn the bird breast upwards, so that it is above the cooking liquid. Cook uncovered for another hour. The bird will be nicely browned and tender enough to cut with a spoon.

CRAB

We don't use crab nearly enough, probably because most cooks
are daunted by the idea of dealing single-handedly with the
beast. But, unless you have a treasure for a fishmonger, who
will only sell the freshest of crabs cooked by himself that
morning, it is always best to cook your own if you can. There
are various ways to do this. Fishmongers often drown them first
in desalinated water. The most humane way to kill them, if you
have the knack, is to turn them on their backs and stab them
with a long awl in the two nerve centres, the first in a vent
behind the tail and the other at a point behind the head. If you
are a first-timer, ask your fishmonger to show you how.
Throwing the crabs into boiling water is no good, as they tend
to shoot their claws, which allows water to ruin the flesh. I go
for the 'bring to the boil in salted water' method, where the
crabs just seem to doze off as the water heats. When the water
is just simmering, cook for 15 minutes for the first 450g/1lb
and 10 minutes for any subsequent same weights.

The RSPCA reckons that since crustaceans cast off shells and
claws with gay abandon – which mammals would certainly
never do with their limbs – there is some doubt as to whether
crustaceans can feel pain at all. Despite this, the RSPCA gives
crabs the benefit of the doubt and suggests not eating them at
all. That, though, would deprive us of one of the most plentiful
and delicious creatures to come from the sea. So harden your
hearts and enjoy. When you have come to grips with your first
one and produced it triumphantly with a home-made shining
mayonnaise, you will find it gets easier and easier.

When buying crab, make sure it feels heavy for its size and
does not rattle with water when shaken. I'm glad to say our
market in Victoria does a thriving trade every weekend.

JP

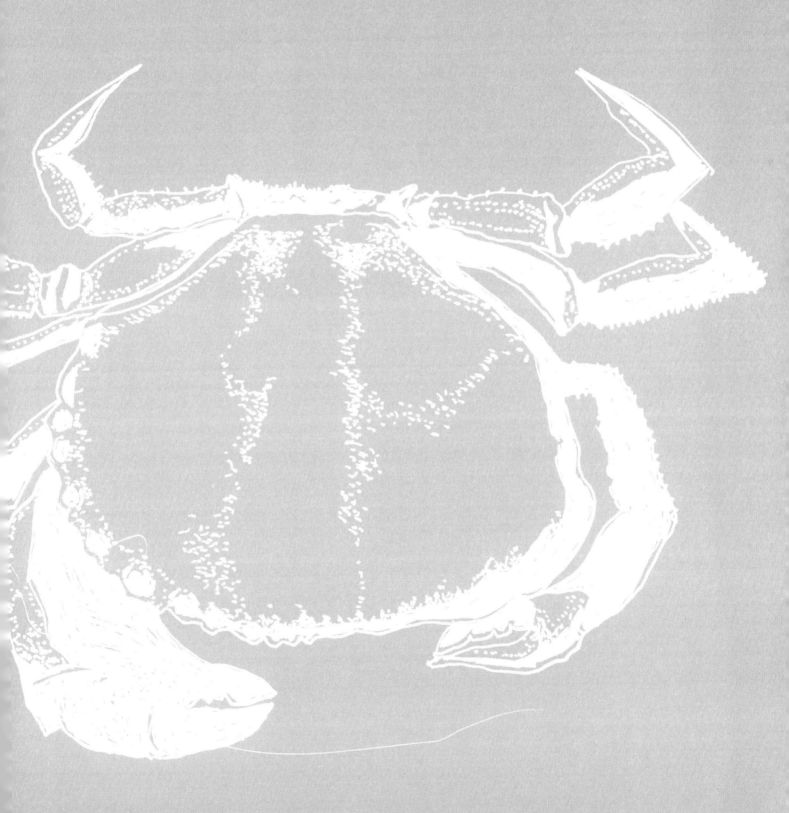

CRAB PROFITEROLES

This is a delicious idea from Karin Perry, good for 'eaty firsties' with drinks or as an hors d'oeuvre. They are excellent piping hot.

175g/6oz unsalted butter
450ml/³/₄ pint water
210g/7¹/₂oz strong white
    bread flour
1 tsp salt
6 eggs, beaten
225g/8oz white crab meat
Pinch of cayenne pepper

Cut the butter into cubes and put it with the water into a heavy pan. Heat gently until the butter melts, then bring to a rapid boil. Quickly tip in the flour. Remove the pan from the heat and beat the mixture violently with a wooden spoon. As soon as the dough is smooth and starts to leave the sides of the pan, add the salt. Set the saucepan in a basin of cold water to cool for 10 minutes.

Gradually stir in the beaten eggs to make a smooth dough. Add the crab meat and cayenne pepper and mix thoroughly into the dough.

Have a greased baking sheet at the ready. Drop dessertspoonfuls of the dough in seried ranks. Bake in a preheated oven at 220°C/425°F/Gas 7 for about 20 minutes – they should be lightly crisp and golden brown in colour. Let them rest for a couple of minutes before serving.

NOTE: If you wish, you can fill them with the brown crab meat, which I think is the best part. Just make a slit in the top of each profiterole with a sharp knife and put a teaspoonful of dark crab meat into the centre.

HOT BUTTERED CRAB

4 medium-sized cooked crabs
1 small clove of garlic
2 anchovy fillets
115g/4oz butter
4 tbsp dry white vermouth
Juice of 1 lemon
Good pinch of freshly grated
    nutmeg
Tabasco sauce

Extract all the meat from the crabs. Wash and reserve the shells.

Finely chop the garlic and anchovies, then fry them gently in a little of the butter for about 3 minutes. Add the vermouth, lemon juice and remainder of the butter, and season with the nutmeg and a good dash of Tabasco to taste. Stir in half of the breadcrumbs and the crab meat. Season with salt and pepper to taste. Stir to blend and cook for about 5 minutes. Add most of the chopped parsley.

55g/2oz fresh white
  breadcrumbs
Salt and freshly ground
  pepper
Small bunch of parsley, finely
  chopped

Transfer the buttered crab mixture to the crab shells, and sprinkle with the remaining breadcrumbs and parsley. Cook under a preheated hot grill until bubbling and browning.

CRAB SOUFFLÉ

This receipt comes from Scotland where the crabs are plentiful and as fresh as can be.

Serves 8–10

Butter and fine breadcrumbs
  for the dishes
85g/3oz unsalted butter
55g/2oz plain flour
450ml/^{3}/4 pint milk
1 bay leaf
100g/3^1/2oz grated onion
Salt and freshly ground
  pepper
1 tbsp anchovy essence
2 tsp Dijon mustard
350g/12oz crab meat (both
  white and brown)
8 eggs, separated

Have ready 2 soufflé dishes or 8–10 individual ramekins. Brush the dishes with soft butter and scatter with fine breadcrumbs, shaking out the surplus.

In a saucepan melt the butter, then stir in the flour and cook gently for 2 minutes, stirring the while. Heat the milk and stir in, little by little, to make a smooth sauce. Add the bay leaf, onion and seasoning to taste. Simmer very gently for about 20 minutes, stirring occasionally.

Remove the pan from the heat and add the anchovy essence, mustard and crab meat. Beat in the egg yolks very vigorously. Whisk the egg whites until stiff. Add one tablespoonful to the mixture and stir in, then gently fold in the rest a little at a time.

Divide the mixture between the dishes. Bake in a preheated oven at 200°C/400°F/Gas 6, allowing 12–15 minutes for the larger soufflés and 7–9 minutes for the smaller ones. Don't peek while cooking. Serve the soufflés immediately.

CRAB BISQUE

This is Richard Shepherd's excellent crab soup from Langan's restaurant in London.

Serves 8

225g/8oz each onion, leek, celery and carrot, all cut into small dice
1–1.3kg/2–3lb whole crabs, shell and claws broken into small pieces and 'dead men's fingers' removed
115g/4oz butter
A bouquet garni of bay leaf, thyme, parsley stalks and peppercorns
115g/4oz tomato purée
8 tbsp Cognac
8 tbsp dry white wine
1-2 litres/2 pints good fish stock
115g/4oz long-grain rice
Salt and freshly ground pepper
120ml/4fl oz double cream

Sweat the vegetables and crab pieces in the butter until the vegetables are tender. Add the bouquet garni, tomato purée, Cognac, wine and stock. Stir and bring to the boil. Then add the rice and simmer for 45 minutes with the lid a little askew.

Strain off the liquid through a fine sieve and reserve. Discard the large tough pieces of crab shell, then pulverise the remaining contents of the sieve into a paste using a blender, processor or even pestle and mortar. Pass this through the sieve to remove any sharp pieces of shell. Add the reserved liquid, return to the heat and bring to the boil again.

Check the seasoning and consistency of the soup, which should be fairly thick. If it is too thin, add beurre manié (2 tsp each of flour and butter, mashed together), whisked into the soup a little at a time. Serve topped with a swirl of cream.

Opposite: Crab Bisque

TRIPE

Because this book is about obsessions and because I have been allowed to choose anything I really love, I have chosen tripe. Tripe is wonderfully digestible and very nutritious. In fact, it was once given to sickly children or invalids. That is probably why I became so fond of it – I was indeed a very sickly child. It seems to have done its trick because I now have the constitution of an ox.

A lot of people were put off tripe in their childhood by being made to eat the rather bland, soggy tripe and onions so beloved of English semi-nursery food. I have to say that I have never liked tripe and onions, but I do love tripe. There are many and various ways of preparing it. It is a substance that takes up flavourings and textures remarkably well.

There is a great British tradition of tripe-eating, especially in the counties of the north of England and the Cockney population of London. I remember once going to a rugby match at Salford Rugby League pitch, and with my tea afterwards having the most delicious pickled tripe with a delicate and splendid flavour. I've never managed to find a recipe for it, although (hint, hint) I have been looking for the last 30 years.

Tripe has become unfashionable nowadays and difficult to get. You can no longer buy raw tripe, because the slaughterhouses will not pass it out due to the legislation. And a great many butchers no longer sell parboiled tripe, although they will get it for you if you ask. You used to be able to buy tripe in supermarkets, although I have not seen it recently. It is perfectly legal; it is not in any way dangerous – if you believe the legislation on BSE and Creutzfeldt-Jakob disease – and it is delicious.

There are a number of different sorts of tripe and any of them can be used in the recipes I give here. I do suggest that you overcome any inbuilt dislike you may have for tripe and try some of them to see how very, very delicious tripe is. I'm sure you will be converted overnight.

CDW

Warranted Cast Steel

Nichols Bros

TRIPE À LA MADRILENA

The title means tripe from Madrid. The Spanish do wonderful things with tripe, and I remember, as a child, the tripe stalls in the market in Madrid selling this particular dish. It has a brilliant colour from the red peppers, tomatoes, Serrano ham and chorizo, and a lovely gelatinous texture from the pig's trotters cooked in the gravy. It is well worth taking the trouble to make. For those of you who don't like traditional tripe and onions, it will completely change your attitude to tripe.

900g–1.2kg/2–2^1/$_2$lb tripe, cut
   into thin strips
2 pig's trotters, parboiled for
   2^1/$_2$ hours and drained
3 tbsp olive oil
1 red pepper, seeded and
   sliced into strips
1 onion, chopped
3 tomatoes, peeled, seeded
   and chopped
225g/8oz Serrano or other
   Spanish ham in a piece,
   chopped into small cubes
1 clove of garlic, chopped
^{1}/$_2$ tsp chilli powder
225g/8oz chorizo sausage
   (I like to use the hot one),
   cut into 5cm/2in pieces
Salt and freshly ground
   pepper

In a large, heavy saucepan simmer the tripe and the trotters together in salted water to cover for 1^1/$_2$ hours or until both are tender. Remove the trotters, separate the meat from the bones and return the meat to the saucepan with the tripe and continue while you make the tomato sauce.

In a frying pan heat the oil and fry the red pepper, onion and tomatoes until the onion is soft. Add the ham, garlic, chilli powder and chorizo sausage, and season to taste. Stir well, then pour this sauce into the stewed tripe pan. By now the original amount of water will be much reduced. Simmer gently for a further 10–15 minutes.

TRIPE À LA MODE ANGOULÊME

This is a more traditional tripe recipe – white tripe cooked with white wine, garlic, shallots and other vegetables, and a calf's foot. (You should easily be able to obtain a calf's foot in any of the Muslim Halal butchers in your area.) It is slow-cooked in an earthenware pot, although you can, of course, cook it in a heavy casserole dish. The recipe I've given takes 12 hours' cooking. You can speed this up, but I recommend that you don't – at least once try it as it is meant to be cooked. It is totally delicious.

3 pieces of pork rind
1 large carrot, sliced
1 large onion, studded
    with 2 cloves
A bouquet garni
20 shallots, chopped
5–6 cloves of garlic, chopped
Salt and freshly ground
    pepper
900g–1.2kg/2–2¹/₂lb tripe, cut
    into 5cm/2in squares
1 calf's foot, large bone
    removed, split, blanched
    and cut into pieces
500ml/16floz white wine
500ml/16floz stock
Plain flour
Oil
Toast for serving

Place the pork rind on the bottom of an earthenware casserole with a tightly fitting lid. On top of the rind, put the carrot, onion, bouquet garni, shallots and garlic, and season with salt and pepper. Add the chopped tripe and the calf's foot. Pour in the white wine and enough stock to cover the mixture.

Make a paste with flour, water and a few drops of oil, and use it to seal the lid on the casserole. Bake in a preheated oven at 130°C/250°F/Gas 1–2 for at least 12 hours.

Strain the sauce into a small pan and reduce it over a high heat. Remove the carrot, onion and bouquet garni from the cooked tripe. Arrange the triangles of toast in a serving dish, enough to cover the bottom. Return the reduced sauce to the tripe and pour the mixture over the toast.

HOT AND SOUR FRIED TRIPE

Sri Owen is a brilliant Indonesian cookery writer. She's also a friend of mine, and I know from private experience that her food is as wonderful as her recipes. This one comes from *Indonesian Food and Cookery*, her award-winning book. One does not think of people in South-east Asia as being consumers of tripe, but in fact tripe is one of the best dishes in many Chinese restaurants. The Indonesians also do it very well. This is a totally unusual tripe recipe with its hot and sour flavourings, but the texture of tripe lends itself very well to the dish.

900g–1.2kg/2–2$^1/_2$lb tripe
5 shallots, unpeeled,
    quartered
3 cloves of garlic, thinly
    sliced
5 fresh red chillies, halved
    and seeded
1 tsp ground ginger
$^1/_2$ tsp ground coriander
$^1/_2$ tsp ground lemongrass
1 tsp brown sugar
Generous pinch of salt
90ml/3fl oz tamarind water
    (see note)
2 bay leaves
240ml/8fl oz oil for frying

Put the tripe into a large saucepan with the shallots, garlic and chillies. Add the ground ginger, coriander and lemongrass, the sugar and salt to the tamarind water. Pour the mixture over the tripe. Add the bay leaves. Bring to the boil and simmer the tripe for 30 minutes.

Leave the tripe to cool in the cooking liquid. When cool, remove and drain the tripe and brush away any pieces of herbs. Cut the tripe into small squares.

Heat the oil in a wok or frying pan and fry the tripe, a few squares at a time, until nicely browned. Drain on kitchen paper.

NOTE: To make tamarind water, soak 15g/$^1/_2$oz tamarind pulp in 6 tbsp of boiling water for 20 minutes, then strain.

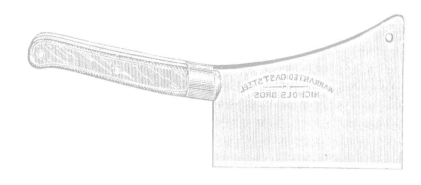

MY ATTEMPTS AT CHINESE TRIPE

When I lived in London I used to go, on my own, to Soho to the Chinese quarter to eat the sorts of things that other people didn't eat, like tripe, duck's webs, pig's maw and other such dishes. There was a restaurant on Shaftesbury Avenue where they cooked the most delicious tripe dish, and I used to go there specifically to eat it. Then one day I came back from a trip abroad to discover to my horror that the restaurant had been bombed by the Triads and completely burnt out. I have never been able to find the same dish again in any other Chinese restaurant. This is my attempt to recreate it. It works quite well, and I hope that you will try it and like it too.

1 tbsp oil (I use half sesame and half olive)

1 bunch of spring onions, roughly chopped

2 cloves of garlic, chopped

2 fresh red chillies, chopped

A thumb-sized piece of fresh root ginger, peeled and chopped into thin strips

1/2 tsp five-spice powder

2 star anise (optional)

900g/2lb tripe, cut into squares

2 tsp soy sauce (use the thick rich variety, not the lighter one)

1 tbsp dry sherry

In a wok or heavy frying pan heat the oil, add the spring onions, garlic, chillies and ginger, and stir-fry briefly. Add the five-spice powder and star anise, if using, and allow to cook for 1 minute, stirring occasionally.

Add the tripe and toss quickly in the oil, cooking for 2 minutes. Add the soy sauce and sherry, and cook briskly over a high heat, stirring constantly, for 2 more minutes. Then cover, turn down the heat and cook for a further 10 minutes. Serve with rice.

EELS

One almost never sees recipes for eels in modern cookery books, which is very sad when you think that at one time eels, being so cheap, were extremely popular with the less well off. Eels were part of everyday fare as far back as the thirteenth century. Shops selling jellied eels and eel pie were once a very common sight in London, but, alas, they have now almost completely disappeared. Eels were used in a festive dish traditionally eaten on Christmas Eve, and were enjoyed at the beginning of a wedding feast when they were cut into elegant fillets.

Eels should always be bought alive – the flesh has a very delicate flavour and texture which, unfortunately, quickly deteriorates. In this day of convenience foods, I'm sure the thought of skinning such an unattractive fish would be daunting to most people. But if you are fortunate enough to find a fishmonger who keeps live eels, it would take just a moment for him to skin this delicious fish for you. If you do the killing yourself and then chop up the eel, be aware that the pieces will continue to jerk about in a rather disconcerting way (I suggest you leave them for a bit in a covered bowl). Avoid eels found in ponds and still waters, as they are inclined to taste a bit muddy.

A really good grilled eel – all crispy on the outside – is a very fine fish. It is a pity, as with many things, that so many people are squeamish about them because they have good firm flesh. Smoked eel, mainly from Holland but becoming more available from our own excellent smokeries, is one of the best of tasty morsels, eaten with some horseradish.

JP

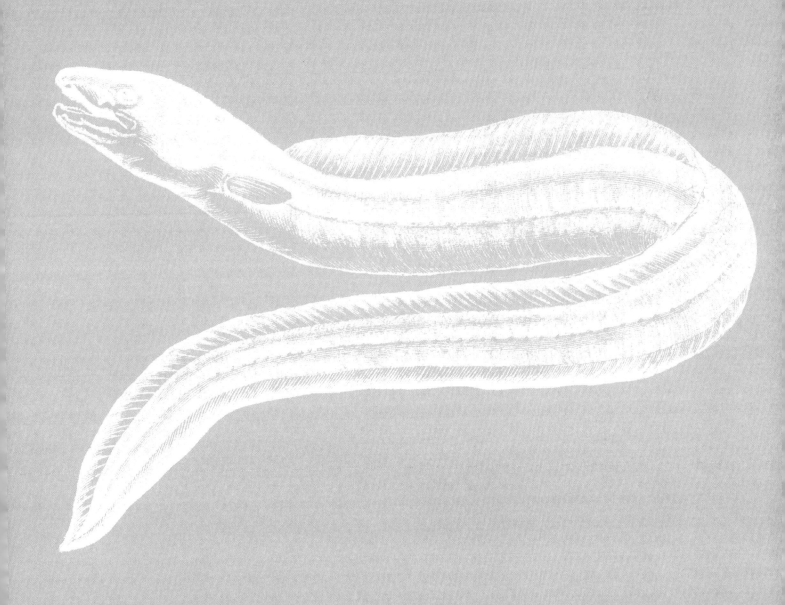

JELLIED EELS

While I'm sure the inclusion of wine is not traditional, I think it does give it a little 'Je ne sais quoi'.

**900g/2lb eel, skinned and
  cleaned**
1 medium onion, finely sliced
2 small carrots, sliced
**A bouquet garni of parsley,
  thyme and bay leaf**
Few strips of lemon rind
5 tbsp white wine
**Small dash of white wine
  vinegar (1–2 tbsp)**
Salt
Black peppercorns
Good fish stock
2 tbsp finely chopped parsley

Cut the eel into 5cm/2in lengths and place in a saucepan with the onion, carrots, bouquet garni, lemon rind, white wine, vinegar, salt and a few black peppercorns. Add sufficient fish stock just to cover the contents of the pan. Bring slowly to the boil, then cover the pan, lower the heat and simmer gently for 1 hour.

Remove the eel with a slotted spoon and place in a pie dish. Boil the cooking liquid to reduce by about one-third. Strain the liquid, add the chopped parsley and pour over the eel. Leave until cold, then chill for several hours to set the liquid.

MARINATED EEL

6 tbsp oil
450g/1lb onions, sliced
2 cloves of garlic, crushed
2 small sprigs of fresh thyme
2 bay leaves
A few black peppercorns
$^1/_2$ tsp salt
**210ml/7$^1/_2$floz white wine
  vinegar**
210ml/7$^1/_2$fl oz water
**900g/2lb eel, skinned, cleaned
  and cut into 7.5cm/3in pieces**
4 tbsp seasoned flour

Heat 4 tbsp of the oil in a saucepan, add the onions and garlic, and cook over medium heat until the onions are soft but not brown. Add the thyme, bay leaves, peppercorns and salt, and pour over the vinegar and water. Bring to the boil and simmer for 20 minutes.

While the marinade is cooking, roll the eel pieces in the seasoned flour. Heat the remaining oil in a frying pan and cook the eel over medium heat for 15 minutes, turning frequently, until they are golden brown.

Transfer the eels to a glass or earthenware dish and pour over the marinade. Cool and then marinate in the refrigerator for at least 24 hours. Serve the eel pieces moistened with a little of the marinade.

EEL PIE

55g/2oz butter
5 shallots, finely chopped
900g/2lb eel, skinned,
  cleaned and boned by
  your fishmonger (weight
  after skinning etc.)
115g/4oz mushrooms, sliced
1 tbsp finely chopped parsley
^{1}/2 tsp finely chopped fresh
  fennel
Grated zest of 1 small lemon
Pinch of freshly grated
  nutmeg
Salt and freshly ground
  pepper
225g/8oz puff or rich
  shortcrust pastry
For the sauce:
25g/1oz butter
25g/1oz plain flour
210ml/7^1/2fl oz fish stock
210ml/7^1/2fl oz white wine

Melt the butter in a frying pan, add the chopped shallots and cook for a couple of minutes to soften. Remove the shallots from the pan with a slotted spoon.

Cut the eels into 5cm/2in slices and flatten slightly. Add to the pan and fry in the butter for a minute or two just to stiffen. Lay the pieces of eel in a pie dish and add the shallots, mushrooms, parsley, fennel, lemon zest, and nutmeg, salt and pepper to taste. Mix gently together.

For the sauce, melt the butter in a clean saucepan, add the flour and cook together for a few minutes, stirring constantly. Gradually add the fish stock and white wine, whisking well. Slowly bring to a gentle boil and cook for 2–3 minutes. Season with a very little pepper and salt. If necessary, add a little more wine or stock as the sauce should not be too thick. Pour the sauce over the eel and leave to cool.

When the filling is cold, cover with the pastry. Bake in a preheated oven at 230°C/450°F/Gas 8 if you are using puff pastry, 200°C/400°F/Gas 6 if you are using shortcrust pastry for about 45 minutes, lowering the heat if the pastry is browning too quickly.

EELS FRIED IN BREADCRUMBS

**900g/2lb eel, skinned,
    cleaned and boned**
1 small onion, thinly sliced
**Salt and freshly ground
    pepper**
8 tbsp olive oil
4 tbsp lemon juice
85g/3oz seasoned flour
2 eggs, beaten
175g/6oz white breadcrumbs

To serve:
Fried parsley (page 54)
Lemon quarters

Cut the eel into 7.5cm/3in pieces. Slightly flatten them, then place in a bowl and sprinkle over the onion slices. Season with salt and pepper, and pour over 4 tbsp of the oil and the lemon juice. Leave the eel pieces in this marinade for about 30 minutes, turning the pieces once or twice.

Remove the eel pieces from the marinade and pat dry. Roll in the seasoned flour, dip in the beaten eggs and, finally, roll in the breadcrumbs to give an even coating.

Heat the remaining olive oil in a large frying pan and fry the eel pieces for about 20 minutes or until they are nicely browned and crisp.

Transfer to a serving dish and decorate with fried parsley and lemon quarters.

NOTE: A bowl of tartare sauce is a good accompaniment to this dish.

EEL EN MATELOTE

70g/2¹/₂oz butter
1 large onion, sliced
1 large carrot, finely chopped
2 cloves of garlic, crushed
A bouquet garni
Salt and freshly ground
    pepper
700–900g/1¹/₂–2lb eel,
    skinned, cleaned and cut
    into 6cm/2¹/₂in pieces
450ml/³/₄ pint dry white wine
12 small button onions
115g/4oz button mushrooms
Beurre manié made with
    55g/2oz butter and
    40g/1¹/₂oz plain flour
    mashed together

Melt 55g/2oz of the butter in a wide saucepan and, when foaming, add the onion, carrot and garlic. Sauté until golden but not brown. Add the bouquet garni and season with salt and pepper. Place the eel pieces on top and pour over the wine – there should be sufficient just to cover the fish. Bring to the boil and simmer for 20–25 minutes.

Meanwhile, cook the onions in boiling salted water until tender. Drain and keep hot. Sauté the mushrooms in the remaining butter. Keep hot.

Remove the eel with a slotted spoon and place in a serving dish with the button onions and mushrooms. Strain the cooking liquid into a clean saucepan and, if necessary, reduce by rapid boiling. Then simmer, gradually adding the beurre manié in small pieces, whisking well between each addition, to slightly thicken the sauce. Pour the sauce over the eel and serve garnished with fried croutons.

NOTE: If preferred, red wine can be used in this recipe.

SALMON

When I was a child, salmon was a luxury. You got it in the fishmonger if you were lucky. My father had friends who fished and they sent us salmon which used to arrive in strange woven bags filled with bog mrytle to keep the flies away. If one was lucky and the weather had not been too hot, the salmon had kept fresh. My father had one friend, a Scottish doctor, who always served his salmon surrounded by a wreath of laurel to honour the great champion fish and the fight that it had put up. This was slightly depressing to me then, but now that I'm older I do see the point.

One never thought of doing much more than poaching salmon and serving it hot with hollandaise or cold with mayonnaise, because it was such a luxury. In historical times this was not always the case. Both the London and the Edinburgh apprentices are recorded as having rioted because they did not wish to be served salmon more than three times a week! Today, with the introduction of farmed salmon, we are much restored to that situation. Salmon is cheap and commonplace, and sometimes extremely nasty.

There is nothing wrong with good farmed salmon, which should be a nice even pink, but not too Barbara-Cartland pink – it was probably fed nasty chemicals to make it that colour – nor too white. Having said that, I was once at a fishmongers when they received a delivery of farmed salmon that was completely white. This was greeted with great delight by the Chinese community, who all bore it away very happily. And, of course, salmon from the areas where there is no shrimp for it to feed on, such as the Baltic, does have white flesh. The advantage of farmed salmon is that it is now cheap enough to be able to do

dramatic things with it, and use strong flavours on it, without feeling guilty that one is in any way impugning the skills of the fisherman.

At Lennoxlove, where I run the catering, I find that salmon is something that people associate with Scotland, so visitors are always looking for it on the menu. This means we can have a lot of variety and amusement in finding different recipes.

CDW

SALMON RILLETTES

Everybody knows pork rillettes, which are found in all charcuteries. This recipe comes from Tessa Hayward's excellent book *The Salmon Cookbook*. It is actually a salmon pâté, but it has the same feel and texture as rillettes. I like it enormously.

2 tbsp olive oil

1 small clove of garlic, cut into 3 or 4 pieces

2–3 sprigs of fresh thyme plus a little extra to garnish

175g/6oz salmon, boned, skinned and cut into cubes

25g/1oz butter

55g/2oz smoked salmon, cut into matchstick pieces

2 tbsp fromage frais or Greek yoghurt

Lemon juice

Salt and freshly ground pepper

Pour the oil into a frying pan and add the garlic and thyme. Heat very gently and just sizzle for about 10 minutes. Do not let the garlic colour or it will leave a bitter taste.

Remove the garlic and thyme from the pan, and add the fresh salmon to the oil. Stir for a minute or two until it is just cooked. Pour the contents of the frying pan into a food processor.

Melt the butter in the pan and add the smoked salmon. The moment it starts to change colour, take the pan from the heat.

Add the fromage frais or yoghurt to the food processor. Process very briefly, just to mix everything. Add the smoked salmon, lemon juice, plenty of pepper and a pinch of salt. Process briefly again, remembering that you want a coarse result at the end. Adjust the seasoning.

Turn into a bowl, which you can line with a piece of foil if you wish to turn out the rillettes. Cover and refrigerate for at least 2 hours. Garnish with a little more thyme before serving.

CEVICHE OF SALMON

The idea of ceviching fish, i.e. 'cooking' it with lemon or lime juice, comes to us from the South American Cervishean tradition. It is a very succulent way of preparing fish, with of course no danger of over cooking. If you are worried about bugs, freeze your fish first.

225g/8oz salmon fillet

175g/6oz lemon sole or plaice fillet

115g/4oz cod or haddock fillet

Juice of 2–3 limes (you can use lemons if limes aren't available)

$1/2$ onion, finely chopped

1 fresh chilli, seeded and finely chopped

1 tbsp coriander seeds, finely crushed

120ml/4fl oz olive oil

Salt and freshly ground pepper

Remove any skin and bones from the fish, then cut them into cubes. Put the cubes into a glass or ceramic dish and pour over the lime juice. Turn with a spoon to coat the fish, then cover and refrigerate for 3–4 hours, turning the fish over after $1^1/2$ hours.

Drain off the juice and combine some of it with the remaining ingredients to make a dressing. Pour the dressing over the fish and refrigerate for another 2 hours.

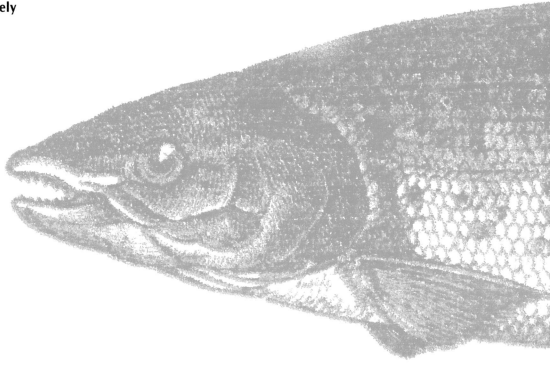

SAKE-MARINATED SALMON WITH COCONUT GREEN CURRY SAUCE

I find bringing a Japanese element into the preparation of salmon works very well.

4 fillets of salmon, 200g/7oz each
3 tbsp olive oil

For the marinade:
A thumb-sized piece of fresh root ginger, peeled and chopped
550ml/18fl oz sake
550ml/18fl oz soy sauce
275ml/9fl oz rice vinegar
8 tbsp soft brown sugar

For the sauce:
2 shallots, finely chopped
25g/1oz butter
275ml/9fl oz fish stock
250g/9oz creamed coconut
25g/1oz green curry paste

In a blender, combine the ginger with the remaining marinade ingredients and blend until smooth. Arrange the piece of salmon in a dish and pour the marinade over, turning the fish to coat well. Cover and marinate in the fridge for a minimum of 3 hours.

Meanwhile, make the sauce. Sweat the shallots in the butter until translucent. Add the stock and curry paste and reduce by half. Add the creamed coconut, stirring well. Simmer for 10 minutes, then pass through a sieve. Set aside.

Remove the fish from the marinade, shaking off any excess. In a heavy flameproof pan, heat the oil until moderately hot but not smoking, and sear the fish on one side only until golden brown – about 3 minutes. With tongs, turn the fish over and put the pan into the middle of a preheated oven at 200°C/400°F/Gas 6. Roast the fish for 4–6 minutes or until cooked through. Serve at once with the heated-through curry sauce.

Previous page: Sake Marinated Salmon

POACHED SALMON WITH HORSERADISH AND APPLES

This is a Russian dish, which is also done with sea bream. It calls for the use of parsley root, which is Hamburg parsley. Unless you grow this yourself, it is not usually obtainable, so you can substitute a small turnip.

A 1.3–1.8kg/3–4lb salmon
240ml/8fl oz white wine vinegar
1 parsley root, cut into pieces
1 heart of celery, cut into pieces
1 leek, sliced
2 medium-sized onions, sliced
Salt
12–15 black peppercorns
2–3 bay leaves
1 lemon, thinly sliced
For the sauce:
3–4 tbsp freshly grated horseradish (do this in a blender)
4–6 cooking apples, peeled and freshly grated
2–3 tsp cider vinegar
Sugar

Place the fish in a dish. Bring the vinegar to the boil and pour over the fish. After a few minutes, remove the fish from the vinegar and transfer to a flameproof casserole.

Put the vegetables in a saucepan with about 600ml/1 pint of water and add the salt, peppercorns and bay leaves. Bring to the boil and simmer for about 15 minutes, when the vegetables will be well cooked. Strain off the liquid and pour it over the fish (discard the vegetables and flavourings). Set the fish to cook over a fairly high heat for about 15 minutes.

To prepare the sauce, mix together the horseradish, apples, vinegar and sugar. Add about 5 tbsp of the strained fish cooking liquid.

Transfer the fish to a warmed serving platter and garnish with lemon slices. Pour over the sauce.

LAMB

As a child of about 8 or 9, I remember stating that when I was a grown-up I would have a leg of lamb a day and a new comic to go with it. Lamb was my favourite meal apart from a chicken's drumstick. We lived in Rye then, and had the most delicious lamb that was grazed on the Romney Marshes, good salt flats which give a distinctive flavour to the meat. Lamb like this is much prized by the French, who have their own agneau pré-salé, grazed on the northern French coastal grasslands, as well as agneau de Sisteron, from the coastal part of the Médoc.

Our splendid lambs first appear in spring, ready for the traditional paschal lamb for Easter Sunday. These come from the winter lambs raised in the south of England. Scottish lowlands lambs come next, followed by the excellent hill-grazing lambs from Wales and Scotland.

A year-old lamb is called a hogget, and after that it becomes mutton – not that you can find mutton anymore unless you have a farmer friend or cousin, as I do. Some people don't like the stronger taste of mutton, but I love it, especially boiled and served with a good caper sauce. It is completely different to a tiny milk-fed lamb. Lamb – or mutton – is one of the most universal of meats, eaten from here to Timbuctoo to the furthest reaches of Outer Mongolia. One only hopes that the animals will always graze naturally and not be given poisonous food by unscrupulous breeders.

During the summer months I particularly like roast lamb cooked to eat cold. When properly done all the juices are retained in the meat and the flesh is pink and moist all the way through, rather than sad and grey-looking as leftover lamb tends to be, only fit for Shepherd's Pie and Pilaffs (these are excellent in their own way, but not like succulent thick slices of pink lamb). I reckon to roast lamb on a grid for 15 minutes to each 450g/1lb and 15 minutes extra. I start the first 15 minutes at 230°C/450°F/Gas 8, then turn down to 180°C/350°F/Gas 4 for the rest of the cooking. Remove from the oven and allow it to cool completely.

I don't like mint sauce with lamb – to my mind it just makes the sweet flesh taste of vinegar, but I do like a lot of chopped fresh mint sprinkled either on the cold slices or over the new potatoes or whatever accompaniment you are planning to serve.

JP

LAMB WITH ROSEMARY, GARLIC AND ANCHOVIES

This is a wonderful family dish, filling the kitchen with its aromas. Evolved from British, French and Italian tastes, it should please every discerning palate.

1 leg of lamb
4–6 heads of garlic
10–12 anchovy fillets
Sprigs of fresh rosemary
1.3kg/3lb fairly waxy
 potatoes (Desirée or the
 like)
2 bay leaves, finely crushed
6 shallots, chopped
Salt and freshly ground
 pepper
Olive oil
300ml/^{1}/2 pint warm stock or
 water
^{1}/2 tsp tomato purée

With a sharp little knife, pierce the lamb with little cuts into the fat and under the skin – about 20 cuts in all. Peel 3 cloves of garlic and cut into sharp little slivers. Insert into the cuts in the lamb. In the bone area, push a piece of garlic, an anchovy and a little sprig of rosemary between the bone and meat. Place the rest of the anchovies across the joint lattice-wise. Set aside in a cool place.

Peel the potatoes and slice quite thinly. Mix with the finely crushed bay leaves and the shallots. Season with salt and pepper. Grease your roasting dish well with olive oil. Arrange the potatoes on the bottom and drizzle with more olive oil. Pour in just enough warm stock or water to cover the potatoes. Cook in a preheated oven at 200°C/400°F/Gas 6 for 1–1^1/2 hours.

Remove from the oven and place the lamb on top of the potatoes. Put back into the oven and continue cooking, allowing 15 minutes to each 450g/1lb of lamb plus 15 minutes extra. Cook at 230°C/450°F/Gas 8 for the first 15 minutes, then turn down to 180°C/350°F/Gas 4 for the remainder.

Meanwhile, peel the remaining garlic cloves, halve them and remove any green shoots. Blanch in boiling water for 3 minutes, then drain.

When the lamb is ready, transfer it with the potatoes to a warm carving dish. Allow to rest for 10 minutes while you put the blanched garlic, remaining stock and tomato purée into the roasting pan with any juices it may contain. Cook on top of the stove, covered, until the garlic is soft. Whizz the lot in a blender, then reheat and pour into a warm jug to serve with the lamb.

AGNELLO CASCE E OVE

This is the Italian version of a lamb fricassee, and very good it is. Culled from the great Anna del Conte, this is a traditional dish from central Italy. You can add some grated horseradish to the final cooking as they do in Venezia Giulia, which is very unusual for Italians, probably an influence from the Austrian Empire.

2 tbsp vegetable oil
1 leg of lamb, about
    1.3kg/3lb, boned and cut
    into 2.5cm/1in cubes
2 tbsp olive oil
1 onion, very finely sliced
1 tsp chopped fresh thyme
150ml/¼ pint white wine
Salt and freshly ground
    pepper
3 egg yolks
3 tbsp freshly grated
    pecorino or Parmesan
    cheese
25g/1oz fresh white
    breadcumbs
Juice of 1 lemon

Heat the vegetable oil in a large frying pan. When really hot, add the meat and brown rapidly on all sides, lifting and turning as you brown. Remove the meat to a side plate.

Put the olive oil and onion into a flameproof casserole large enough to receive all the ingredients and sauté until soft. Add the meat and the thyme and mix well, then pour over the wine. Bring to the boil. Lower the heat to simmering point and season to taste with salt and pepper. Cover and simmer for about 45 minutes or until the lamb is tender.

Beat the egg yolks lightly. Add the cheese, breadcrumbs and lemon juice, and mix all together with a goodly grinding of black pepper. Stir into the lamb and cook gently for a further 5 minutes or until the egg sauce has thickened. Stir all the time to avoid curdling. Adjust the seasoning and serve with little new potatoes, rice or noodles, plus a good salad on the side I should think.

CAWL

I'm including this Welsh recipe for Patricia! Apparently Cawl was originally made with bacon, and fat bacon at that, but now it is usually made with lamb, although there are those aficionados who maintain it should be made with brisket of beef. Cawl was originally the staple diet of poor farmers, and ingredients would vary with the seasons and what was available.

I always start the Cawl the day before so that any fat can be removed. This, of course, was not common practice until fairly recently, and there are still those who maintain that if there are no stars of fat on the Cawl it cannot be a good one! An expression often used by Cawl lovers is that 'Cawl Ail Dwymo' (Cawl twice warmed) is even more delicious.

1.3kg/3lb best end of neck of lamb
2 large onions, sliced
2 medium carrots, cut in chunks
1 medium parsnip, cut in chunks
3 large potatoes, cut in chunks
3 large leeks, sliced
1 large bunch of parsley, chopped
Salt and freshly ground pepper

Cover the lamb with cold water, add half the sliced onion and bring to the boil. Simmer gently for 1 hour. Remove from the heat and leave overnight to get cold, when you can easily remove the fat.

Strain the stock into a clean saucepan, reserving the lamb. Bring the stock to the boil, then add the carrots, parsnip, potatoes, remaining onion, 2 of the leeks and half the parsley. Leave to cook gently for 30 minutes.

Return the lamb to the broth, just to heat through. Add the remaining leek and parsley, and season with salt and pepper. Cook for 5 minutes, and the Cawl is ready to serve.

NOTE: Celery, cabbage and even Brussels sprouts can be added when available. I like to add 25–55g/1–2oz of pearl barley with the vegetables, to slightly thicken the broth.

Opposite: Navarin Printanier (see page 158)

NAVARIN PRINTANIER

This is an excellent spring stew, to be made when the lambs are gambolling and the ravishing little baby turnips – an essential part of this dish – are just appearing. You don't often find a navarin in British restaurants, but it is a fine family dish.

1.3kg/3lb boneless lamb

3 tbsp olive oil

2 tsp sugar

Salt and freshly ground
    pepper

2 tbsp plain flour

600ml/1 pint lamb or beef
    stock

2 tbsp tomato purée

2 plump cloves of garlic,
    crushed

Sprigs of fresh rosemary

2 bay leaves

12 small pickling onions or
    shallots

12 little new potatoes, peeled

12 little baby turnips,
    quartered

12 young carrots, quartered

225g/8oz green beans

225g/8oz shelled peas

Whatever meat from the lamb you are using (you can mix them if you so wish), remove all excess fat and any hard bits of skin. Any bits of bone can be kept to be added to the stew for greater flavour, and removed after cooking. Cut the meat into 5cm/2in cubes and blot with kitchen towels.

Heat the olive oil in a big frying pan until very hot but not smoking, then brown the lamb cubes rapidly on all sides. Do not crowd the pan, but brown a few pieces of lamb at a time, removing them with a slotted spoon into a waiting flameproof casserole. When they are all browned and in the casserole, sprinkle them with the sugar and toss over a moderate heat for 3–4 minutes until the sugar has caramelised. Season with salt and pepper, and add the flour. Toss again to brown the flour, mixing it well with the lamb.

Remove any fat from the frying pan, then pour in the stock. Bring to the boil, scraping any goodies from the pan as you do so. Pour over the lamb in the casserole. Add the tomato purée, garlic, herbs and, if necessary, additional stock or water just to cover the meat. Bring to simmering point, then cover and cook for 1 hour. If you prefer cook in a preheated oven at 180°C/350°F/Gas 4 for 45 minutes.

Pour the contents of the casserole into a colander or large sieve set over another pan. Remove any bones and return the meat to the rinsed-out casserole. Skim the fat from the stewing liquid, season to taste and pour back over the lamb.

Cut a little cross on the base of each onion to ensure even cooking. Add to the casserole together with the potatoes, turnips and carrots, and mix with the lamb and sauce. Bring the contents of the casserole to the boil, then lower the heat, cover and simmer gently until everything is cooked and tender, about 45 minutes.

Prepare the beans and peas by dropping them into a pan of boiling water and cooking for 5 minutes, then drain and rinse under cold water. Add them to the lamb stew 5 minutes before serving. Serve the stew with some good French bread and a bottle of robust red wine.

WALNUTS

In Gascony, on the 24 June, they take the young walnut shoots and put them into eau-de-vie, to make a delicious liquor. Maybe it is because 24 June is my birthday that I feel such an affinity to walnuts. Looking like wizened little creatures, with a resemblance to the human brain, they have always been among my favourite things. I love their delicious sweetness and texture.

I remember as a child feeling incredibly frustrated that I couldn't crack two walnuts together in my hands like my father could. And even when I used the rather strange nutcracker in the shape of a ship's wheel that we had at home, I still seemed to be unable to get the walnut meat out of the shell.

Walnut trees come to us from Persia, now Iran. There you see them growing on the hills above Egry Vicavir. There is a sense of romance about them. In England the walnuts that grow in the garden very seldom ripen, and even less so in Scotland. However, one can still make delicious pickled walnuts and other preserves from them.

There is a strange and sadistic rhyme that goes: 'A wife, a dog and walnut tree/The more you beat them/The better they be.' Clearly one doesn't wish to encourage beating either women or dogs, but it is actually true that if you beat a walnut tree it loosens the bark and helps stimulate the sap to rise.

CDW

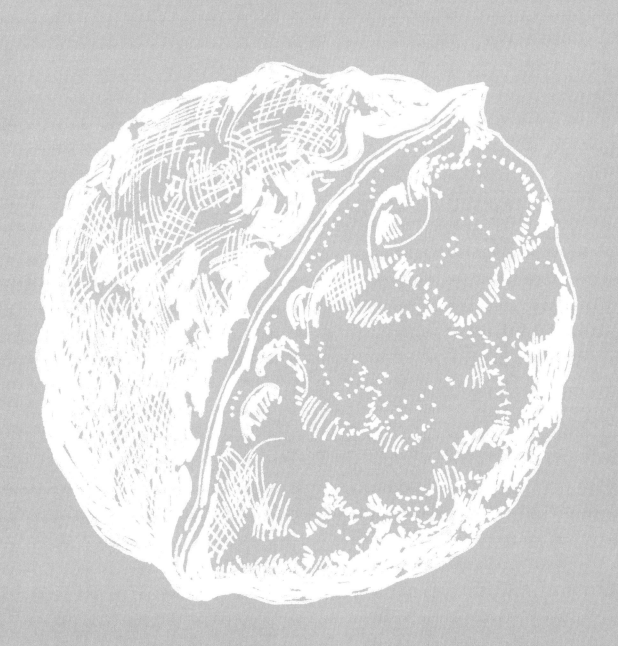

LENTIL AND WALNUT LOAF

This may smack heavily of the vegetarian – indeed it is a vegetarian dish – but it is extremely good, lovely on a cold lunch table with cheese or a salad. It is particularly delicious with a little carpaccio of beef.

450g/1lb lentils
450g/1lb tomatoes, peeled,
    seeded and coarsely
    chopped
Salt and freshly ground
    pepper
Juice of ½ lemon
225g/8oz shelled walnuts
1 large strong onion,
    chopped
1 tsp dried sage
1 egg, beaten
2 tbsp salad oil

Cook your lentils according to type and packet instructions until they are tender. Meanwhile, put the tomatoes in a saucepan with a little water and seasoning, and allow them to reduce to a rough sauce. Add the lemon juice and reduce again.

Drain your lentils and put them in a food processor together with all the other ingredients including the tomato sauce. Whiz together until you have your desired consistency. Turn into a loaf tin and bake in a preheated oven at 180°C/350°F/Gas 4 for about 45 minutes. Turn out and serve warm.

WALNUT, HONEY AND POPPYSEED SALAMI

This looks exactly like one of those rather strange German salamis when it is finished. It is, however, an extremely sweet but very delicious Hungarian pudding. It is quite economical for a buffet or a row of puddings, and very easy to make providing you take a little time. Not a lot can go wrong.

Makes 24–30 pieces

350g/12oz honey
175g/6oz poppyseeds, slightly
    mashed with a pestle and
    mortar

Put the honey into a double boiler, or a bowl set over a pan of boiling water, and bring to the boil (this is slower than using an ordinary saucepan, but safer because it prevents any danger of the honey burning). Remove the honey from the heat and mix in the

350g/12oz ground walnuts
Pinch of ground cloves
1/2 tsp ground cinnamon

poppyseeds, walnuts and spices. Leave the mixture to cool.

Place the mixture on a marble slab or wet board and shape it into a salami-like cylinder. Roll it in greaseproof paper and refrigerate overnight. Cut into slices just before serving.

GÂTEAU DE MORUE DE ST VINCENT

This is a traditional French celebratory dish, eaten on the feast of St Vincent. The combination of walnuts and salt cod is excellent.

700g/1 1/2lb salt cod
450g/1lb potatoes
115g/4oz shelled walnuts, crushed
1 clove of garlic, crushed
325ml/11fl oz walnut oil
6 eggs, separated
Chopped fresh thyme
Chopped parsley
Freshly ground pepper

Soak the salt cod for 12 hours, changing the water frequently. Then put it in a pan, cover with fresh cold water and bring slowly to the boil. Take off the heat and leave it in the water to swell and poach for 15 minutes.

Boil the potatoes in their skins, then drain and peel. Mash them very smooth.

Drain the fish thoroughly. Skin, bone and flake it. Add it to the mashed potatoes together with the walnuts, garlic, oil and the egg yolks. Season with a little thyme and parsley and pepper to taste. Whisk the egg whites and fold into the mixture.

Pour into a lightly oiled soufflé dish or round cake tin and bake in a preheated oven at 180°C/350°F/Gas 4 for 40 minutes. Serve hot.

WALNUT PANCAKES

This is a Hungarian walnut dish, very rich, very delicious, very straightforward. I once 'had' (I can't think quite how else to describe it) a Hungarian trapeze artist. He had an enormously sweet tooth and pined for the puddings of his childhood. He would have loved this. It is quite a lengthy recipe to prepare, but well worth the effort.

For the pancakes:
3 eggs
300g/10oz plain flour
240ml/8fl oz milk
1 tsp sugar
Pinch of salt
240ml/8fl oz carbonated
    water
Clarified unsalted butter for
    cooking

For the filling:
4–6 tbsp single cream
115g/4oz caster sugar
2 tbsp rum
225g/8oz ground walnuts
55g/2oz raisins, chopped
1 tsp grated orange zest

For the chocolate rum sauce:
115g/4oz good plain
    chocolate, grated
200ml/7fl oz milk
3 egg yolks
2 tbsp sugar
2 tbsp cocoa powder
1 tbsp melted butter
2 tbsp light rum

Mix together the eggs, flour, milk, sugar and salt to make a smooth pancake batter. Let it rest for 1–2 hours.

Stir in the fizzy water just before cooking the pancakes. Heat a 20cm/8in frying pan. When the pan is hot add $^1/_4$ tsp clarified butter and heat it, tilting the pan so the butter covers the bottom. Pour in a ladleful of batter and gently tip and twist the pan so that the batter covers it completely. When the top of the pancake bubbles, turn it over and cook for 4–5 seconds on the other side. Remove the cooked pancake. As they are made, stack the pancakes, putting greaseproof paper between them.

To make the filling, bring the cream to a simmer and add the sugar, rum, walnuts, raisins and orange zest. Simmer over a very low heat for 1 minute. Adjust the texture by adding either more cream or more ground walnuts.

Put a heaped teaspoon of filling in the centre of each pancake. Fold in four instead of rolling. Sauté the folded pancakes in clarified butter in a large shallow pan for a few minutes on each side. Arrange the pancakes, overlapping, on a warm serving dish. Keep hot.

For the sauce, melt the chocolate in the milk over a low heat. Whisk in the egg yolks, then remove from the heat. Add the sugar, cocoa, butter and rum, and stir until smooth. If the sauce is too thick to pour, add a little more milk. Pour the sauce over the pancakes and serve at once (two pancakes per person).

NOTE: If you wish, you can flambé the pancakes.

LEMONS

Another of my desert island choices – if they are not already growing there – has to be the lemon. Think of all the fish I will catch and grill – if I didn't have lemons it would be a sorry kettle of fish. Lemon juice would be useful for any wild pigs I might catch or birds of the air. It's also good for the skin and useful as an antiseptic for wounded feet and the like. And there are bound to be some other forms of fruit or coconuts on the island (unless I am on an ice floe, God forbid!) which wouldn't be hurt by a drop of lemon juice.

What could be nicer than to sit in a ravishing lemon grove surrounded by the dark green leaves, the beautiful fruit and, curiously enough, the blossom also appearing for the next year's growth? They are the prettiest trees of all when in such a state. On a hot day nothing could be better than an ice-cold Spremuta di Limone squeezed from lemons growing at your elbow. We used to take bunches of lemon leaves, with their wonderful scent, and put them in the bath before running the hot water over them. The whole bathroom would be infused with this splendid essence. Such a treat.

Curiously enough, lemons don't thrive in most tropical countries. There they will use limes instead, which are much stronger. But the Middle East seems able to produce lemons and they use them a lot preserved in salt. We can now get preserved lemons over here, and they are a delicious accompaniment to many spicy dishes.

The great thing about lemon juice is that it enhances so many foods. The zest, which must always be cut really thinly, also gives a fantastic flavour to many meat, fish or fruit dishes. It is particularly splendid, I think, in gremolata, which is a mixture of chopped parsley, garlic and lemon zest, scattered over Osso Bucco. The combination of the smells is heady and perfect for the rich meat and risotto.

Never throw away squeezed lemon halves, but keep them for the day by the sink. Then you can use them to remove fish or onion and garlic smells from your fingers. Or you can stick them on your elbows while you are reading a book, to soften and whiten your skin.

JP

COD FILLETS WITH LEMON SAUCE

4 thick cod fillets
1 large clove of garlic,
**   creamed**
Juice of 1 small lemon
Salt and freshly ground
**   pepper**
120ml/4fl oz olive oil
15g/¹/₂oz butter
2 tbsp finely chopped shallots
3 medium tomatoes, peeled,
**   seeded and chopped quite**
**   small**
1¹/₂ tbsp finely chopped
**   parsley**
Dash of dry white vermouth –
**   about 2 tbsp**

Rub the fillets with the garlic, 1 tbsp of the lemon juice and some salt and pepper. Leave for 30 minutes.

Brush an oven dish with a little olive oil and put in the cod fillets.

Melt the butter in a small frying pan and soften the shallots over a low heat so that they do not brown. Add the tomatoes and cook together for another few minutes. Pour this mixture over the cod fillets. Sprinkle the parsley over the fish, then pour over the remaining olive oil and lemon juice and the dry vermouth.

Cover the fish with greaseproof paper and cook in a preheated oven at 200°C/400°F/Gas 6 for 15 minutes. Remove the greaseproof paper and cook for a further 15 minutes or until the fish is cooked. Serve with the cooking juices poured over the fish.

SPICY LEMON POTATOES

450g/1lb potatoes
4tbsp olive oil
2 heaped tsp garam masala
1 heaped tsp turmeric
2 large cloves garlic, finely
chopped
2tsp finely grated fresh
ginger
Grated rind and juice of half
a large lemon
Salt
Freshly ground black pepper

Scrape potatoes (or peel if necessary) and cut into large chunks. Where possible I like to use two large potatoes, each weighing about half a pound. Cut each potato into four pieces. Boil potatoes for five minutes then drain and leave to cool slightly.

Pour olive oil into an ovenproof dish and place in a pre-heated oven 400°F/220°C/Gas 6 until hot. Meanwhile mix garam masala and turmeric together and roll potatoes in this mixture until well covered. Add potatoes to the hot oil together with the lemon, garlic, ginger and seasoning and cook in the centre of the oven for 45-60 minutes.

Check on potatoes during cooking and stir gently to ensure that potatoes are browning evenly.

LAMB WITH EGG AND LEMON SAUCE

2 tbsp plain flour

Salt and freshly ground
  pepper

900g/2lb lean boneless lamb,
  cut into 4cm/1^1/2in chunks

25g/1oz butter

1 tbsp olive oil

1 small onion, finely chopped

2 cloves of garlic, crushed

2 tsp finely chopped fresh
  sage

1 bay leaf

210ml/7^1/2fl oz dry white
  wine

600ml/1 pint chicken stock

2 small lemons

2 egg yolks

Finely chopped parsley to
  garnish

Season the flour with salt and pepper and sprinkle over the lamb cubes. Melt the butter with the oil in a large frying pan. Add the lamb and fry over fairly high heat until the cubes are golden brown. Transfer to a flameproof casserole using a slotted spoon.

Lower the heat under the frying pan and cook the onion and garlic until the onion has softened. Add the sage, bay leaf and wine. Bring to the boil, scraping the bottom of the frying pan to incorporate any brown bits. Continue to boil until the wine is reduced by half, then stir in the stock and bring back to the boil. Pour the contents of the frying pan over the lamb in the casserole.

Cover and place in a preheated oven at 150°C/350°F/Gas 4 and cook for 1^1/2 hours or until the lamb is tender.

While the lamb is cooking, finely grate the zest from 1 lemon and squeeze the juice from both. Beat together the lemon zest and juice with the egg yolks.

Remove the casserole from the oven. Add 2 tbsp of the hot gravy to the egg and lemon mixture and mix gently together. Add another 2 tbsp of the gravy to the mixture and stir again, then whisk the mixture into the casserole. Place the casserole over a moderate heat and cook for about 1 minute or until the sauce has thickened slightly. Sprinkle with chopped parsley and serve.

HERRINGS WITH LEMON AND MUSTARD SAUCE

2 tbsp plain flour
Salt and freshly ground
    pepper
1 large egg
1 tbsp milk
2 tsp French mustard
4 large herrings, filleted
55g/2oz butter
For the sauce:
2 tbsp lemon juice
4 tbsp olive oil
$^2/_3$ tsp French mustard
1 clove of garlic, creamed
2 tsp chopped fresh chives

Season the flour with salt and pepper. Beat the egg with the milk and the mustard. Rinse and dry the herring fillets. Dip into the beaten egg mixture and then in the seasoned flour.

Melt the butter in a large frying pan and fry the fillets over a moderate heat for 3–4 minutes on either side and until a light golden brown.

Meanwhile, to make the sauce, whisk together all the ingredients, except the chives, and taste for seasoning. Add the chives just before serving, with the herring.

LEMON CURD

115g/4oz unsalted butter
225g/8oz caster sugar
Finely grated zest and juice
    of 2 large or 3 small
    lemons
3 eggs, beaten

Put the butter, sugar and the lemon zest and juice into a double saucepan, or into a bowl set over a saucepan of barely simmering water. Stir the mixture with a wooden spoon until the sugar has completely dissolved.

Remove the pan from the heat and strain in the beaten eggs. Replace the saucepan over a low heat and stir the contents until the mixture thickens and coats the back of the wooden spoon. Pour into warm jars and seal.

HEAVENLY PIE

3 eggs, separated
$^1/_2$ level tsp cream of tartar
225g/8oz caster sugar
Grated zest of 1 lemon
Juice of 1 small lemon or
$^1/_2$ large lemon
200ml/7fl oz double cream,
whipped
Few large black grapes

Whisk the egg whites with the cream of tartar until stiff, then gradually whisk in 85g/3oz of the caster sugar. Continue whisking, and when whites are very stiff and glossy fold in a further 85g/3oz of the sugar.

Lightly butter a 7in pie plate and spoon on the meringue, spreading in a level layer. Bake in the bottom of a preheated oven at 130°C/250°F/Gas 1–2 for 1–1$^1/_2$ hours.

Put the egg yolks, the remaining sugar and the lemon zest and juice into a bowl and beat well together. Set the bowl over a saucepan of gently simmering water and cook, stirring constantly, until the mixture thickens. A little patience is needed as the mixture must not be allowed to get too hot. When the mixture is thick, remove from the heat and allow to cool until just warm. Fold in $^1/_2$ tbsp of the whipped cream. Spread the mixture over the meringue base.

When the pie is completely cold, spread on the remaining cream, forking it into swirls. Decorate the edge of the pie with skinned, halved and seeded black grapes.

ROSE PETAL JAM

The old fashioned, heavily-scented, dark red roses are best for this. Use an average sized cup.

4 cups of rose petals
3 cups of sugar
3 cups of water
2 tbsp lemon juice

Carefully rinse the rose petals and snip off white bases. Place the petals in a bowl and gently mix in half the sugar. Cover the bowl and leave overnight.

The next day, put the remaining sugar and the water on to boil, stirring to dissolve the sugar. Add the lemon juice and boil for a further 5 minutes.

Leave aside to cool until just warm, then stir in the rose petals. Put back on the heat and bring slowly to the boil. Boil gently until thick, then pour into hot jars and cover in the usual way.

FIGS

When I was a child I could never understand why Adam and Eve wasted their time picking an apple, when clearly from the fact that they wore fig leaves they must have had access to figs. I first tasted figs as a small child in Bordagira, where we were staying on a friend's property. I thought that the delicate pink and white flesh of the fig was one of the most delicious things I had ever eaten. I have other favourites now, but still love figs. That moment when the taste of the fig explodes in your mouth is quite exquisite. And the fig is one of the most sensual-looking fruit – there is something about it that has a hint of wickedness, which fits again with my query about the Garden of Eden: why lose your virtue for an apple?

In my childhood home we had a fig tree that produced, every year, small fruit which didn't ripen. And then came the first really hot summer, and I discovered that it is only sun that is needed to make figs ripen. Because the season for fresh figs is so short, it is more common to get them in a dried or preserved state. This is a fine way to enjoy them, as the natural sugar in the fig lends itself particularly well to drying, bottling, canning and any other manner of preserving. Valvona and Crolla, the famous Italian delicatessen in Edinburgh, produces fig balls for Christmas every year, which are figs pressed together and roasted in the oven to dry them out. They are presented wrapped in fig leaves, and are delicious, sticky and pretty. When the fig balls start appearing in the shop, it is one of the signs to me that I'm coming to the end of my working year and will soon be able to collapse in a heap.

I have tried to give you recipes for both fresh and preserved figs and I hope you will like them as much as I do.

CDW

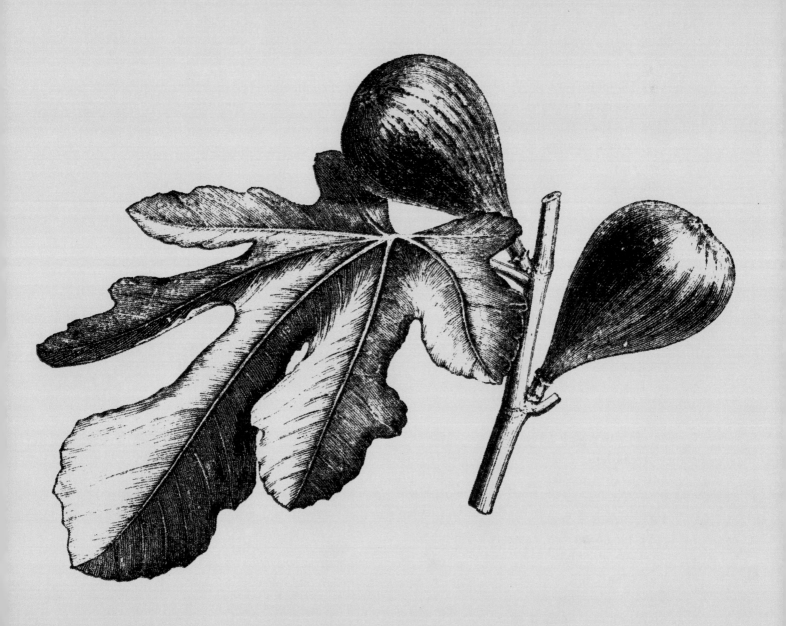

FIG IN PEARATRICE

I'm often in the situation that I have to prepare a pudding for surprise guests, only to find that the only thing I have in my cupboard is a box of dried figs. This is my secret recipe for such occasions, an easy pudding that is absolutely delicious and succulent. When served hot with rich cream it takes an awful lot of beating. It also impresses your drop-by guests who hadn't really expected anything very special.

450g/1lb large, plump Californian dried figs
115g/4oz toasted, blanched almonds, chopped
Honey
240ml/8fl oz port wine

Separate the figs and place them in a steamer over a little boiling water. Steam until plumped. Remove from the heat.

While the figs are cooling, mix the almonds with enough honey to bind together, keeping the mixture rather dry.

When the figs are cold enough to handle, open up each one, without actually separating it, and stuff with the almond mixture. Place the stuffed figs in a shallow pan and pour over the port wine. Heat thoroughly without boiling, basting the figs occasionally with the wine. Serve hot with whipped cream.

FIG BREAD

This is a good, rich bread, delicious eaten with cheese or just with butter by itself.

Makes 1 loaf

800g/1³/₄lb strong white bread flour
4 tsp baking powder
¹/₂ tsp salt
115g/4oz caster sugar
300g/10oz dried figs, coarsely chopped
2 eggs, beaten
350ml/12fl oz cold milk
55g/2oz butter, melted

Combine the flour with the baking powder, salt and sugar, and sift over the chopped figs. Blend well to coat the figs with the flour mixture (this will prevent them from falling to the bottom of the bread). Mix the eggs with the cold milk and add to the flour and fig mixture, mixing thoroughly. As you go along, add the melted butter and stir in.

Turn the dough into a generously greased loaf tin and allow to stand for 25 minutes to mellow and ripen.

Bake in a preheated oven at 180°C/350°F/Gas 4 for 1 hour. Turn out on to a wire rack and allow to cool.

Opposite: Fig in Pearatrice

DUKE OF HAMILTON'S FIG ICE-CREAM

In the winter of 1997, my friend Angus Hamilton was sent a letter by a man who was compiling recipes from all the great aristocratic houses. Angus passed this to me, and we discussed what would be best. He was very keen that I should do something using the brown figs from the fig tree that grows against the front wall of Lennoxlove House, his family home. The figs never fail to ripen, despite the Scottish climate. This was in November, so I had to wait until the following year before figs were available. Angus Hamilton is very fond of ice-cream, so I decided to make a fig ice-cream, which is not as easy as it sounds, because figs do not have a very strong intrinsic flavour. However, this recipe is the result of my efforts. I hope you like it as much as I did.

Makes 1.2litres/2 pints

500ml/16fl oz milk
A large piece of liquorice root
1 vanilla pod, split open lengthways
210g/7¹/₂oz granulated sugar
6 egg yolks
250ml/9fl oz double cream
4 preserved figs, cut into pieces (the ones that you find in jars with brandy will do very nicely for this)
6 fresh figs, cut into pieces

Place the milk, liquorice, vanilla pod and half the sugar into a saucepan. Bring to the boil. Once it has boiled, cover and remove from the heat. Leave to stand for 10–15 minutes before proceeding.

Put the egg yolks and remaining sugar in a bowl and beat until the mixture thickens and forms a ribbon.

Remove the liquorice and vanilla pod from the milk, place over a high heat and bring back to the boil. Pour a little of the boiling milk into the bowl with the egg yolks and sugar, whisking constantly as the milk is added. Move the saucepan from the heat and pour the contents of the bowl into it, stirring constantly with a wooden spoon or spatula. Return the saucepan to a low heat and, stirring carefully, allow to form a custard. If you are using a thermometer, this should reach 85°C/185°F. However, the more usual test is to lift the wooden spoon and run your finger, in a line, across the film of cream that adheres to it. If the custard is properly cooked, it will nicely coat the spoon and the top end of the line will hold its shape. When the custard is cooked, it should be removed from the heat immediately.

Pour into a bowl and add the double cream, stirring constantly to mix well. The finished cream must now be allowed to cool completely, before being placed in the ice-cream machine. To speed the cooling, place the bowl in a larger bowl that has been filled with ice cubes and water. The cream should feel cold to the touch when it has finished cooling.

Once the cream is completely cold, pour it into the ice-cream freezer and start the machine. Churn for 1 minute, then add the preserved figs. Continue to churn according to the instructions on your model. When the ice-cream has finished churning, remove it from the machine to a freezerproof container. At this point stir in the fresh figs. Allow to freeze, and serve with more fresh figs on the plate.

CRYSTALLISED FIGS

If you have fig trees you will have a lot of figs, and there is also a time in good years when you can buy figs quite cheaply. Crystallised figs in shops are fairly expensive and often of rather dicey quality, so it is much nicer to make your own, and amaze your friends.

50 fresh figs
500g/1lb 2oz granulated
    sugar
200ml/7fl oz water
Caster sugar to finish

Choose figs that are just ripe and in good condition. Prick them with a fine needle.

Dissolve the granulated sugar in the water in a large pan and then cook until the syrup begins to bubble (110°C/230°F/Gas 1). Place the figs carefully into the syrup, which will increase in volume, and heat until the syrup begins to bubble again. Remove the figs with a slotted spoon and leave them on a tray overnight. Reserve the syrup.

The next day, return the syrup once more to the heat and, when it begins to boil, add the figs. Cook until they absorb almost all of the syrup. Transfer them to a tray lined with greaseproof paper and leave to dry in the sun, covered with gauze. When they are completely dry, roll in caster sugar and then store.

COFFEE

When I first went to Sicily one of my favourite things was sitting in a shaded cafe enjoying a delicious Granita di Caffé or coffee water ice, served in a long tall glass with a dollop of whipped cream on the top. It was my idea of heaven. The granita is made with very strong espresso coffee, well sugared and then frozen into granules. The effect of the sweet coffee coming through the ice granules, with the whipped cream, is particularly enchanting, rather like a crème de menthe frappé.

Coffee is really one of my favourite ingredients, but it must be the very finest quality. For me, the continental blend gives the best results. Some people may find it too strong, but that's what I like. I find coffee is the best flavour for ice-cream – far better than all the other new-fangled concoctions – and it is especially nice if sprinkled with some finely ground coffee, which gives a nutty texture.

According to a snippet from Claudia Roden: 'It was the priests in Italy who appealed to Pope Clement VIII to have the use of coffee forbidden among Christians. Satan, they said, had forbidden his followers, the infidel Moslems, the use of wine because it was used in the holy communion and given them instead his "hellish black brew". It seems the Pope liked the drink, for his reply was: "Why, this Satan's drink is so delicious that it would be a pity to let the infidels have exclusive use of it. We shall cheat Satan by baptising it." Thus coffee was declared a truly Christian beverage by a far-seeing Pope.' So you can thank Rome for a godsend to us all.

JP

GRANITA DI CAFFÉ

85g/3oz sugar plus an extra 2 tsp
450ml/³/₄ pint hot, strong espresso coffee
240ml/8fl oz double cream, whipped

Add the sugar to the hot coffee and stir until completely dissolved. Leave it to cool, then pour it into an ice-cream machine and freeze according to the manufacturer's instructions.

If you have no machine, do as they have done in Italy since time immemorial: pour the mixture into a shallow freezer container (it used to be in an old-fashioned ice-cranker) and freeze for about 30 minutes, stirring around the edge occasionally until it is just beginning to set. The mixture should be slushy. Serve in glasses topped with whipped cream or panna montata.

BURNT COFFEE

This is an interesting little offering from Eliza Acton. It is probably the forerunner to the Irish Coffee, but not as rich as no cream is added. In France it is rather vulgarly called Gloria. Heaven knows why, but someone will doubtless tell me.

Make as much strong coffee, as clear as possible, as you may need. Sweeten it in the cup with white sugar, almost to a syrup, then pour brandy on the top, gently, over a spoon. Set fire to it with a lighted paper and, when the spirit is, in part, consumed, carefully blow out the flame. Then drink the Gloria quite hot.

COFFEE NUT CAKE

175g/6oz self-raising flour
A pinch of salt
3 eggs
175g/6oz margarine
175g/6oz caster sugar
1 tsp instant coffee granules
2 tsp hot water
25g/1oz walnuts
For the icing:
1 tsp instant coffee granules
    plus extra to decorate
2 tsp hot water
55g/2oz unsalted butter,
    softened
115g/4oz icing sugar
40g/1¹/₂oz walnuts for
    decoration

First grease two 18cm/7in sandwich tins and line the bottom of each with greaseproof paper.

Put the flour, salt, eggs, margarine and caster sugar in a bowl and beat together with a wooden spoon for about a minute. Dissolve the coffee in the hot water, then stir this and the walnuts into the cake mixture. Divide the mixture evenly between the tins. Bake in a preheated oven at 170°C/325°F/Gas 3 for 25 minutes. When they are done, turn the cakes out and cool on a rack.

To make the icing, dissolve the coffee in the hot water, then simply cream together with the butter and sugar.

Spread half the icing on one cake and sandwich together with the other. Spread the rest of the icing on top. Decorate with the walnuts and sprinkle with the coffee granules.

COFFEE MOUSSE

It always seems strange to me that the British don't really have a passion for coffee-flavoured puddings. I have always preferred them to all others, ever since childhood when our beloved cook used to make what seemed to me enormous coffee cakes for my birthday. They were usually decorated with little eggs as it was always around Easter. Here is a splendid coffee mousse that I hope you will all try. It is nice and simple to make and, I think, a boon to any table.

3 leaves of gelatine
4 tbsp hot, strong coffee
3 egg yolks
130g/4^1/$_2$oz caster sugar
1 tbsp coffee liqueur
300ml/^{1}/$_2$ pint double cream,
  lightly whipped
4 egg whites

To decorate:
Whipped cream (optional)
Ground coffee

Put the gelatine to soak and melt in 2 tbsp of the hot coffee.

Place the egg yolks and the sugar in a bowl with the remaining coffee. Set the bowl over hot water and whisk until the mixture is thick and fluffy – almost falling in ribbons. Add the gelatine mixture and whisk until cool. Then whisk in the coffee liquor. Leave in a cool place.

When the mixture is on the point of setting, fold in the cream and stiffly whisked egg whites. Pour the mixture into a dainty bowl or soufflé dish and allow to set in the fridge.

Decorate with piped cream, if you like, and scatter over fine ground coffee grains.

RASPBERRIES

Agreeable as I find strawberries, with their jolly, lascivious taste and look, my true love is the raspberry. I wait for them every year like a small child, eager with anticipation. They join asparagus, gull's eggs and the first lobster as the highlights of my year. When the first raspberries appear, I rush home to eat them with thick golden, oozing cream, pressing them against the roof of the mouth so that they explode into flavour. The best raspberries undoubtedly come from Scotland, with the Blairgowrie region of Perthshire producing the most. Sadly, the Scottish raspberry is at present under threat from cheap, inferior fruit from Central Europe, which is not the native breeding ground of the raspberry.

The red strawberry is a bred fruit in the sense that it is a combination of yellow Virginian strawberries merged with red South American strawberries, to produce the red heart-shaped fruit that we know so well. There are different varieties of raspberry. Indeed, the Americans produce one that is almost black in colour, whilst the French produce both yellow and white raspberries. But they are all natural species – they have not been hybridised in the way that strawberries have. That is why one gets raspberries in season and now gets strawberries all the year round, from all sorts of strange and terrifying places.

Raspberries need to ripen on the vine, and be sensitively and delicately picked or they will go off. They therefore rate as a luxury fruit, and not one that can be easily grown out of season, although there has been successful experimentation with growing them in polytunnels in Arbroath, which has produced very successful fruit as late as October – the wind that damages them so easily is excluded and there is still enough natural light and sunshine to grow them.

When buying raspberries look at the underside of the punnet. If there is any sign of staining you will know that the fruit has already begun to go off at the bottom. It is difficult to get a punnet of raspberries without at least one or two mouldy ones. Extract the healthy fruit from the punnet with a toothpick to prevent any further handling.

CDW

RASPBERRY AND CHOCOLATE MILLEFEUILLES

You can either buy the puff pastry ready-made or use the recipe in our first book, *Two Fat Ladies.*

450g/1lb puff pastry

A bar of Valhrona or other good white chocolate

600ml/1 pint double cream, whipped

3 punnets of raspberries

Roll out the pastry on a floured surface to a large rectangle and trim to 45 x 30cm/18 x 12in. Cut it into three strips, each measuring 30 x 15cm/12 x 6in. Place each pastry strip on a baking sheet and leave to stand for 10 minutes (this is important, because puff pastry bruises easily and the standing time allows it to recover from the rolling out). Then bake it in a preheated oven at 230°C/450°F/Gas 8 for 15–20 minutes or until it is well risen and golden brown. Cool on wire racks.

Gently melt the white chocolate, either in a bowl set over boiling water or in a microwave. White chocolate burns very easily and will not temper, so be very careful with it.

To assemble the millefeuilles, place one pastry rectangle on a plate and pour a layer of white chocolate over it. Spread with whipped cream and add a layer of raspberries. Place a second pastry rectangle on top and layer on more of the white chocolate, whipped cream and raspberries. Place the final piece of pastry on top of this and decorate with the remaining chocolate, cream and raspberries, this time arranging the raspberries in a nice pattern.

FROZEN RASPBERRY SOUFFLÉ

225g/8oz granulated sugar
4 tbsp water
8 egg yolks
450ml/³/₄ pint double cream
85g/3oz caster sugar
225g/8oz raspberries

Heat the granulated sugar with the water until dissolved, then boil until the syrup will fall into a long thread from a spoon (110°C/230°F if you are using a sugar thermometer).

Beat the egg yolks lightly with a fork in the top of a double boiler or bowl set over a pan of hot water. Add the hot syrup very slowly, stirring constantly with a wooden spoon. Cook in the top of the double boiler for 4-5 minutes, stirring frequently, until the sauce has the consistency of thin mayonnaise.

Whip the cream and fold in the caster sugar. Crush the raspberries with a fork and mix with the cream. Combine the two mixtures, folding together thoroughly.

Choose a soufflé dish or other round, deep serving dish that is a little too small for the amount of mixture. Line the sides of the dish with a piece of greaseproof paper that comes 2cm/³/₄in above the rim. Fill the dish with the mixture and place in the coldest part of the refrigerator to set.

Before serving, trim off the paper rim and the dessert will look like a hot baked soufflé. Serve immediately.

RASPBERRY WHIPPED CREAM

1 egg white
115g/4oz icing sugar
150g/5oz raspberries

Whisk the egg white until stiff enough to hold its shape, then whisk in the icing sugar. Mix in the raspberries.

NOTE: You can dust the whip with shredded blanched almonds or crumbled macaroons, if you wish.

RASPBERRY AND REDCURRANT JAM

I'm too mean with my raspberries to use all of them up in jam, so I mix them with redcurrants. This has a wonderful colour. The flavour of the raspberry is dominant, and there are still lots left to eat.

700g/1¹/₂lb raspberries
700g/1¹/₂lb stripped
   redcurrants
600ml/1 pint water
1.3kg/3lb preserving sugar

Prepare the fruit and put in a preserving pan. Add the water and simmer gently until quite tender – this should only take 4–5 minutes.

Remove the pan from the heat, add the sugar and stir until it has dissolved. Return the pan to the heat.

Boil rapidly, stirring frequently to prevent sticking, and skimming when necessary. To test for setting, either use a sugar thermometer, which should reach a temperature of 110°C/230°F. Or use the saucer test: put a little jam on a cold saucer and allow it to cool, then push your finger across the top of the jam; the surface will wrinkle when a set has been obtained.

Remove from the heat and allow the jam to cool, stirring frequently to prevent the fruit from rising to the top. Then fill sterilised jars to the rim (the jam will shrink a little). Cover the surface of the jam with a waxed disk, wax side down, making sure that it lies flat and that there are no air bubbles trapped. Make a lid for the jar by covering the top with damped cellophane held in place with a rubber band. Remember to label the jars with the name and date, and store in a cool dry place away from the light.

CREAM

How can people be so ungrateful not to embrace cream into their diets? It is one of the most natural and God-given ingredients for texture and sumptuousness in sweets, puddings and a hundred different sauces. It enhances practically anything you might care to cook. A great dollop of whipped cream on top of either a pudding or a strong soup is always a treat. I'm sure, if not gobbled every day, cream can do you no harm, but will only enhance your life.

I don't know if they still do it, but one of the great treats in the days of rationing was to have friends in Cornwall who would sometimes send you lovely little tins of fresh clotted cream. This was usually eaten, with cries of delight, on hot scones with raspberry jam. Clotted cream seems to be an entirely British affair – I've certainly never seen it anywhere else.

Cream was consumed at all levels of society in Tudor times. Among the creamy dishes of the Tudor and Stuart period were trifles, fools and white pots. An Elizabethan trifle was made thus: 'Take a part of thick cream and season it with sugar, ginger and rose water. So stir it as you would, then have it and make it luke warm in a dish on a chaffing dish and coals. And after put it into a silver piece or bowl and so serve it to the board.'

During the next centuries cream ceased to be part of a rural man's banquet, where once it was consumed with strawberries and other berries. Toffs thought this might be rather rich for the stomach, and instead, among the more well-to-do, cream was added increasingly to made dishes and sauces. Whereas the most sumptuous medieval fare had been marked by its content of spices, sugars, dried fruit and wine, that of the eighteenth century was rich with butter and cream.

It is significant that the word cream or creme is used figuratively for the very choicest part of something, which itself is very choice, as in crème de la crème. It's even used in advertisements for secretaries. So away with all this nonsense about cholesterol, which is a very modern invention and only harmful to a few unfortunates. After all, if a receipt has a pint of cream in it, it is probably enough for 10 to 12 people.

JP

SCRAMBLED EGGS AND SMOKED SALMON

This is a recipe that at one time was very popular as a starter to a dinner party, but now, sadly, seems to have lost favour.

8 fresh eggs
210ml/7^1/$_2$fl oz double cream
Salt and freshly ground
   pepper
25g/1oz butter
175g/6oz smoked salmon,
   diced
Few cooked asparagus tips,
   warmed in butter
Chopped fresh chives

Beat the eggs with half of the cream and salt and pepper to taste. Melt the butter and add the eggs, stirring constantly. When the eggs are beginning to thicken, add the smoked salmon. Cook for another minute or two, being careful not to overcook.

While the eggs are cooking, heat the remaining cream in a small pan.

Spoon the eggs on to a warmed serving dish. Pour the hot cream over them and garnish with the asparagus tips and chopped chives. Serve immediately.

CUCUMBER SAUCE

One of the simplest, but one of the best sauces with cold salmon or lobster.

¹/₂ cucumber, finely diced
300ml/¹/₂ pint double cream
450ml/³/₄ pint white wine
vinegar
Salt and freshly ground
pepper

The diced cucumber should be allowed to drain in a sieve for 30–45 minutes before making the sauce, so that the excess juices are removed. Otherwise they will seep into the sauce and spoil the consistency.

Whip the cream, gradually adding the white wine vinegar as you do so. Fold in the cucumber, and season with salt and pepper. Chill until ready to use.

CREAM OF CAULIFLOWER SOUP

One of the simplest, but one of the best sauces with cold salmon or lobster.

55g/2oz butter
2 large or 4 small leeks,
white part only, sliced
1 large potato, peeled and
roughly chopped
1 stick of celery, chopped
1¹/₂ pints chicken stock
1 medium cauliflower,
broken into florets
300ml/¹/₂ pint single cream
Salt and freshly ground
pepper
A little freshly grated nutmeg

Melt the butter in a saucepan, add the leeks, potato and celery, and cook over gentle heat for 10–15 minutes. Pour over the stock and add most of the cauliflower florets, reserving a few for garnish. Bring the contents of the saucepan to the boil and cook until the vegetables are tender. Allow to cool slightly.

Meanwhile, cook the reserved cauliflower florets in boiling salted water until just al dente. Drain and keep warm.

Purée the soup in a blender or food processor, then return to the pan and add cream to give the desired consistency. Season with salt, pepper and nutmeg. Gently reheat the soup, then stir in the reserved florets. Serve with some crisply fried croutons.

PETITS POTS DE CRÈME

5 egg yolks
1¹/₂ tbsp caster sugar
2 tbsp strong black coffee, cold
2 tsp Tia Maria (optional)
450ml/³/₄ pint double cream
To serve (optional):
A little whipped cream
Chocolate curls

Whisk the egg yolks with the sugar, coffee and Tia Maria, if using. Scald the cream and stir into the egg yolk mixture. Strain into a jug, and pour into small ramekin or cocotte dishes.

Stand the dishes in a baking tin and pour in hot water to come half-way up the sides of the dishes. Cover the tin with foil and place carefully in the centre of a preheated oven at 150°C/300°F/Gas 2. Cook for about 30 minutes or until firm.

Remove carefully from the oven. Leave to cool, then chill before serving. Decorate with a little whipped cream and a few chocolate curls, if desired.

BOODLES FOOL

A favourite recipe from the famous Boodles Club in St James Street.

Grated rind and juice of 2 small oranges
Grated rind and juice of 1 small lemon
1 level tbsp caster sugar
1 tbsp Cointreau
10fl oz double cream
4-5 trifle sponges, depending on the size of the bowl

Combine the juice and rind of the oranges and lemon. Add the sugar and stir until the sugar has dissolved. Then stir in the Cointreau.

Cut the trifle sponges in half and arrange them in the bottom of a glass trifle bowl, preferably one with straight sides. Pour the cream into a large bowl and whip until it is just beginning to thicken. Take care not to over whip the cream. Then gradually add the orange and lemon juice while continuing to whip the cream.

Pour the cream mixture over the sponge cakes and chill in the fridge for 3-4 hours.

CHOCOLATE

People tell me that chocolate affects the same part of the brain as sex. That explains people's passionate addiction to it, though personally I've never really found that there was much of a competition – of the two, sex is infinitely preferable. However, I do have a very soft spot for chocolate, and no doubt in my declining years it will be some sort of compensation prize.

I did, however, once work for a woman who was so besotted with chocolate that she would ring me up in the middle of the night to ask me if I knew whether there was any chocolate in her house or if I had any chocolate about me. And sometimes, in extremis, she would send me down, long after closing, to the village shop or pub to buy her some chocolate. It was in the days of my drinking, and she would say to me: 'I understand about your gin. It is just like me and chocolate.' So perhaps there's something in it after all.

Chocolate is a product of the New World. It came to us via Spain and Portugal as a savoury – one of the earliest chocolate recipes is for rabbit cooked with chocolate. The South American and Central American Indians made a sort of paste of their bitter chocolate, which they may have eaten for reasons of sexuality or sensuality. I've never been quite sure, but I cannot imagine that unsweetened chocolate is anything to write home about. However, once chocolate was brought to the Old World, to be united with that miracle of nature, sugar, everything changed. There is no doubt that the combination of chocolate, sugar, cream and all the other lovely things, is very indulgent and irresistible indeed. If you put out puddings on a pudding sideboard, you will find that the ones containing chocolate almost invariably get attacked first.

Chocolate is still added to savoury dishes like Coq au Vin, and there is no doubt that a little bit of unsweetened chocolate does lift that type of dish quite surprisingly. It is also very good with hare, bringing out all the full richness of the blood and gaminess of that delicious animal.

The thing to look out for in chocolate, so I'm told, is cocoa solids – the more cocoa solids the chocolate has the better quality it is. Speaking as someone who has a sneaking liking for good old-fashioned milk chocolate made by Cadbury's, I sometimes feel that chocolate snobs are on a par with wine snobs. However, having said that, there can be no doubt at all that when it comes to cooking, the more cocoa solids you get, and the purer the chocolate, the better the result. There is something so rich and lavish and sensuous about a really dark chocolate mousse made with superb chocolate.

The best chocolate truffles I've ever eaten are made by Sally Clarke at her delicatessen in Kensington Church Street, London. In fact, so good are they, they have completely ruined me for any other type of chocolate truffle at all, on which I can only look disdainfully. This is probably just as well, as there is a tendency to put alcohol in chocolate truffles, which of course I no longer consume.

Here I have tried to choose chocolate recipes that run the whole gamut of deliciousness and variety.

CDW

CHOCOLATE PYE

This is a recipe from Hannah Glasse dating from the eighteenth century. The crackling crust is particularly successful – it looks beautiful and is delicious to eat.

For the crackling crust:
175g/6oz ground almonds
1 egg white
55g/2oz caster sugar
For the topping:
225g/8oz plain chocolate,
    grated
300ml/¹/₂ pint double cream

To decorate:
Toasted almonds
Yellow rose petals

Work the ground almonds, egg white and sugar into a paste and knead into a ball. On a sugared surface, roll out to a round large enough to line a 20cm/8in non-stick flan tin, ¹/₄ inch thick and leave to dry for 30 minutes. Then place in the tin and decorate the edges with the finger and thumb technique. Line with foil (but no baking beans) and bake blind in a preheated oven at 180°C/350°F/Gas 4 for 20–25 minutes. Watch carefully to avoid scorching. Leave to cool.

Melt the chocolate in a bowl set over hot water, then mix in the cream, stirring all the time to prevent splitting. Remove from the heat and, as the chocolate starts to set, beat the mixture to a light foam. Allow to cool for a minute or two before pouring into the cooled crackling crust. Leave to set. Serve decorated with toasted almonds and yellow rose petals.

CHOCOLATE PARFAIT

I do like a nice parfait. It is not quite an ice-cream and perhaps less of an effort to eat. Use the best possible chocolate for this recipe, with 70% cocoa solids or more.

6 tbsp water
115g/4oz sugar
Pinch of salt
225g/8oz bitter dark
    chocolate, grated
2 egg yolks, well beaten
Scant 1 tsp powdered
    gelatine
240ml/8fl oz double cream,
    whipped until stiff
1¹/₂ tsp pure vanilla extract

Put 4 tbsp of the water in a saucepan with the sugar and salt. Bring to the boil, stirring to dissolve the sugar, then boil to make a syrup that will split into a thread when dipped from the tip of a spoon.

Melt the chocolate in a bowl set over hot water. When smooth, add to the syrup a little at a time, stirring constantly. Pour the chocolate syrup in a fine stream on to the egg yolks, beating briskly and constantly as you go.

Soften the gelatine in the remaining cold water, then set in the pan of hot water to dissolve, stirring until it does so. Add the gelatine to the chocolate mixture, stirring in well so that it does not form lumps. Allow to cool, stirring occasionally.

Fold in the whipped cream and the vanilla extract. Churn in an ice-cream machine. Or put into a refrigerator tray and freeze, stirring with a fork from time to time as you go.

CHOCOLATE MARSHMALLOW ICE-CREAM

This is a nice old-fashioned American ice-cream recipe which I got from my great-aunt Jessica. It is rich and gooey, and rather sickly – just everything that an ice-cream should be. You serve it scooped into a crown and fill the centre of the ring with raspberry whipped cream.

55g/2oz bitter chocolate, grated
225g/8oz milk, freshly scalded
16 marshmallows, cut into small pieces
Plain flour
Scant ¼ tsp salt
4 tbsp granulated sugar
240ml/8fl oz undiluted evaporated milk
1 tbsp lemon juice
½ tsp ground cinnamon
Raspberry whipped cream (page 190) to serve

Put the chocolate in a bowl set over hot water and melt. Remove from the heat. To the melted chocolate add the scalded milk slowly and gradually, stirring constantly until the mixture is thoroughly blended. Dip the marshmallows in flour and add to the chocolate mixture with the salt and sugar.

Set the bowl over the hot water again and heat slowly, stirring constantly, until the marshmallows have melted and the sugar dissolved. Leave to cool, then chill.

Whip the evaporated milk with the lemon juice and cinnamon until thick. When the chocolate and marshmallow mixture is cold, fold in the whipped evaporated milk. Freeze in a tray, without stirring, for 3¼ hours.

To serve, use a tablespoon dipped in hot water to rapidly scoop egg shapes from the frozen ice-cream and arrange like a crown on a well-chilled platter. Fill the centre with raspberry whipped cream.

Overleaf: Chocolate Pye

CHOCOLATE CHILLI BISCUITS

The Mexicans regarded chocolate as a savoury rather than a sweet commodity, and ate it cooked in casseroles – undoubtedly mixed with chilli. This is a whimsical little recipe, combining both sweetness and the traditional chilli-chocolate Mexican idea. I like it. I hope you will.

250g/9oz Mexican chocolate (if you can get it) or a good dark chocolate, grated
4 tbsp water
900g/2lb plain flour
115g/4oz cocoa powder
2 tsp chilli powder, preferably ground ancho chilli
1 tsp ground cinnamon
^{1}/4 tsp cayenne pepper
^{1}/4 tsp salt
175g/6oz unsalted butter, at room temperature
300g/10oz caster sugar
1 tbsp pure vanilla extract
2 eggs
115g/4oz icing sugar

Put the chocolate and water in a small saucepan and stir over a low heat until the chocolate melts, about 2 minutes. Set aside. Sift together the flour, cocoa powder, chilli powder, cinnamon, cayenne and salt, and set aside.

Beat together the butter, caster sugar and vanilla extract in a large bowl until well mixed. Beat in the eggs and the chocolate. Add the dry ingredients in two or three batches, beating well after each addition to make a somewhat moist dough. Divide the dough into four equal parts.

On a lightly floured surface, roll each portion of dough into a log approximately 30cm/12in long and 4cm/1^1/2in thick. Place the dough logs on a sheet of greaseproof paper, cover loosely with another sheet of paper and refrigerate until firm but not hard (1^1/2–2 hours).

When ready to bake the biscuits, slice the logs into 5mm/^{1}/4in thick rounds and arrange on ungreased baking sheets. Bake in a preheated oven at 180°C/350°F/Gas 4 for about 6 minutes or until light brown and crusty round the edges. Turn the biscuits over, and bake for a further 8 minutes or until no longer moist in the centre.

Remove from the oven and cool on the baking sheets for about 5 minutes, then transfer to a serving platter. Sift over the icing sugar and serve right away, or store in an airtight container.

BRAZO GITANO

This is a Spanish cake, one that used to be made for me by my mother's Spanish domestic couple, Ferdinand and Isabel. The name always intrigued me as a child, and I still love the richness of the recipe.

For the sponge cake:
5 large eggs, separated
Finely grated zest of 1 lemon
100g/3¹/₂oz caster sugar plus extra for sprinkling
Pinch of salt
4 tbsp plain flour

For the filling:
115g/4oz dark chocolate, broken into small pieces
3 large egg yolks
1 tbsp plain flour
2 tbsp cornflour
¹/₄ tsp ground cinnamon
300ml/¹/₂ pint milk
100g/3¹/₂oz sugar
¹/₂ tsp pure vanilla extract
4 tbsp rum

Take a 38 x 26cm/15 x 10¹/₂in Swiss roll tin and line it with non-stick baking paper. Grease the paper well with butter.

Put the egg yolks, lemon zest and half the sugar in a bowl and whisk hard until the mixture looks like thick, pale custard. This should take 2–3 minutes. In another bowl, whisk the egg whites with the salt until soft peaks form. Gradually add the remaining sugar and whisk to a glossy meringue. Fold the meringue into the egg yolk mixture, cutting down with the side of a large metal spoon. Sift some of the flour over the top and fold in. Continue to fold in the flour a little at a time.

Pour the cake mixture into the prepared tin and bake in a preheated oven at 180°C/350°F/Gas 4 for 12–15 minutes or until pale golden brown and springy to the touch.

Sprinkle a piece of baking paper with caster sugar. Turn the cake directly on to the sugared paper and remove the lining paper. Roll up the cake with the sugared paper inside. Wrap in a dampened tea towel and leave to become cold.

For the filling, melt the chocolate in a bowl set over hot water, stirring occasionally. Mix the egg yolks, flour, cornflour and cinnamon together to make a paste, adding a little of the milk if needed. Bring the rest of the milk and the sugar to boiling point in a heavy-based saucepan and pour on to the yolks, stirring continuously. Return to the pan and cook over a low heat, stirring, until the custard is thick and smooth (it will be lumpy at first). Remove from the heat, and stir in the chocolate, vanilla and rum. Leave until cold.

Unwrap the sponge, unroll it and remove the paper. Spread with the chocolate filling and reroll. Keep wrapped in the paper in the fridge until it is needed. Serve the same day.

APPLES

I suppose we must consider Adam and Eve as the first great PR people for apples. Never has a fruit been blamed for so much. I have to say, though, what a curious fruit to conjure up the fatal temptation that led to original sin and the expulsion from the Garden of Eden. I always feel that it probably wasn't an apple at all, but something bitter like a quince or crab apple that dealt the fatal blow. Of course, why then would Eve have found it so delicious? I suppose it could be because it was forbidden.

However, since then apples have been regarded as a delight. Some have the most exquisite taste, although the greatest disappointment is finding a beautiful specimen, only to discover, on first bite, that it has no taste at all and a furry texture. Regrettably, like much else, they are often grown now more for appearance than flavour. However, we still retain in Britain some of the best apples in the world. The monks in Ampleforth have over 50 varieties of tenderly tended fruit, blessed by the Lord no doubt.

I remember when we lived on the little River Mole, near Hampton Court, we had a fine old-fashioned orchard of both eating and cooking apples. The trees hadn't been pruned or looked after for several years during the War, but their fruit had a taste far surpassing that of any shop-bought specimens of a much greater size. The apples used to be kept in the cellar all through the winter. Before this, when the fruit was still on the trees, naughty little boys used to climb our walls for obvious pilfering purposes. This gave us children enormous sport, as we would lie in wait for the boys until they crossed the wall with their booty. Then we would pepper them on their behinds with our airguns, creating shrieks from the miscreants and great joy for ourselves. We would probably be arrested or sent for counselling in this modern age, but we had such fun. The risks were well known on both sides.

JP

SNOW CREAM

This is a modern version of a ravishing Georgian delicacy, resurrected from Margaretta Acworth's 200-year-old book of receipts. This pretty pudding should be allowed to stand an hour or more before you intend to serve it. The meringue appears to float on the cream and, as the dish is left to stand, the cream runs in rivulets into the meringue and forms a light crust in places.

225g/8oz cooking apples, such as 1 large or 2 small Bramley's
Grated zest and juice of 1 large or 2 small lemons
4 egg whites
115g/4oz caster sugar
120ml/4fl oz double cream
1/2 tsp orange flower water (found in any good chemists)

Put the apples whole into a saucepan and cover them with cold water. Bring to the boil, then simmer gently until they are tender. Drain. When the apples have cooled, cut them into quarters and scrape the flesh away from the skin and cores. Measure 115g/4oz of the apple flesh into a mixing bowl or food processor.

Add the lemon juice, egg whites and most of the sugar (reserve 1 tbsp to add to the cream). Beat or whiz all the ingredients together vigorously for about 5 minutes, until they form a stiff froth that will hold its shape like a meringue. Refrigerate until ready to serve.

Pour the cream into a separate bowl and mix in the orange flower water, grated lemon zest and remaining sugar. Leave it to stand in the fridge for 1 hour or more.

Spoon the meringue mixture on to a serving dish (choose a dish with a good brim or raised edge). Gently pour the cream around it. Serve with macaroons or amaretti.

APPLE PANDOWDY

I remember, as a teenager, hearing this song on the American Forces Network and always thought it sounded very jolly:

'Shoo Fly Pie and Apple Pandowdy
Makes your eyes light up
And your tummy say "Howdy!"'

So I thought we should include the pandowdy in our apple feast.

900g/2lb cooking apples
2 tbsp golden syrup
¹/₂ tsp ground cinnamon
¹/₄ tsp freshly grated nutmeg
175g/6oz plain flour
Good pinch of salt
2 tsp baking powder
115g/4oz sugar
115g/4oz unsalted butter,
  melted
Generous 150ml/¹/₄ pint milk

Peel, quarter and core the apples, then thinly slice them into a bowl. Add the syrup, cinnamon and nutmeg, and toss gently to coat the apple slices evenly. Spoon the mixture into a buttered 1 litre/2 pint ovenproof, deep-sided dish.

Sift the flour, salt and baking powder into a bowl and stir in the sugar. Make a well in the centre and add the melted butter and the milk. Stir to make a smooth batter, then spread it evenly over the apple slices.

Bake in a preheated oven at 180°C/350°F/Gas 4 for 40–45 minutes or until the sponge topping has risen and is browned. To serve, you can invert the pudding on to a dish or serve from the baking dish. It is, of course, highly improved with cream in generous dollops.

APPLE HONEY CRISP

900g/2lb cooking apples,
    peeled and sliced
1 tbsp lemon juice
4 level tbsp honey
55g/2oz plain flour
55g/2oz rolled oats
85g/3oz soft brown sugar
Good pinch of salt
85g/3oz unsalted butter

Lightly grease a 1 litre/2 pint ovenproof dish. Arrange the apples in the dish and sprinkle the lemon juice over them all. Spoon the honey over the fruit.

In a bowl mix together the flour, oats, sugar and salt. Rub in the butter until the mixture resembles breadcrumbs. Sprinkle the crumbs evenly over the fruit.

Bake in the centre of a preheated oven at 190°C/375°F/Gas 5 for about 40 minutes or until the apples are tender and the topping is browned. Serve with single cream (Surprise! Surprise!) and eat hot.

APPLE TANSY

Another old favourite. This receipe is no longer flavoured by the bitter herb tansy, which gave it its name, but by a splendid combination of spices and rose water, more appealing to modern tastes.

4 eggs, separated
150ml/^{1}/$_4$ pint double cream
Pinch of ground cinnamon
Pinch of freshly grated
    nutmeg
Pinch of ground ginger
115g/4oz caster sugar
1 tsp rose water
450g/1lb dessert apples
55g/2oz unsalted butter

To serve:
Sugar
Grated orange zest

Beat together the egg yolks, cream, spices, sugar and rose water until smooth. Whisk the egg whites until stiff and fold them into the mixture. Peel, core and slice the apples, and fold them in.

Melt the butter in a frying pan and pour in the apple mixture. Fry for about 6 minutes or until the underside is set and golden brown. Then put the pan under a preheated hot grill for 2–3 minutes. Serve hot, sprinkled with sugar and grated orange zest.

Opposite: Apple Tansy

BUTTER

Some time ago I had a dinner party for which I bought some proper butter, made in a proper churn and stored in a wooden crock, from Iain Mellis, the very good cheesemongers in Victoria Street in Edinburgh. I put it on my dinner table and people helped themselves to it without noticing, until one friend said, 'They don't make butter that shape any more'. Then I was able to explain that they did and that that was how butter ought to be, and what good butter it was.

We are quite lucky in this country with the quality of even the average everyday butter that is sold on our shelves. To my taste too much salt is added to English and Welsh butter and this is not something that appeals to me. But the texture and quality of the butter is of a much higher standard than that of a lot of other countries. Also, there is no extraneous water that needs to be pressed out of it when you are beating it. In series three, 'Two Fat Ladies' went to a Welsh farm where we made butter. It was fascinating to see how the milk was churned and churned until the butter began to deposit, and then how the buttermilk was drained off and the butter washed repeatedly and then rechurned and the water patted out of it. It was a long and quite arduous process, but the butter that it produced was totally delicious.

The natural colour of butter, unless the cows have been feeding on buttercups, is white. It is one of those curious anomalies that somebody somewhere along the line decreed that butter should be yellow. So a chemical derived from carrots is added to butter to give it its yellow colour.

Nowadays we are told that butter is bad for us and that we should either eat olive oil – which is good and no doubt very beneficial, but not much of a guard against the cold nights of winter – or margarine or one of those horrible half-fat substitutes. When I was 21 my godfather, who was the head of

Unilever, made me promise that I would never eat margarine, because one didn't know what went into it. That is a promise I've always kept. I do not like margarine. I don't like the smell of it nor its texture, and I'm highly suspicious about what goes into it.

On the other hand, the great smell and feel of butter just fills me with hunger. Butter left in the pan after cooking carries the flavour of whatever you cooked in it, and it is something I tend to scrape up and eat happily. The nicest way to cook a piece of fish is just to put butter on it. A steak cooked with butter is an exquisite thing. Butter enhances sauces of all types and natures. And just slathered on to bread it is a treat in itself. But it must be good, expensive butter.

My advice is, wave two fingers at the pundits and eat lots of butter.

CDW

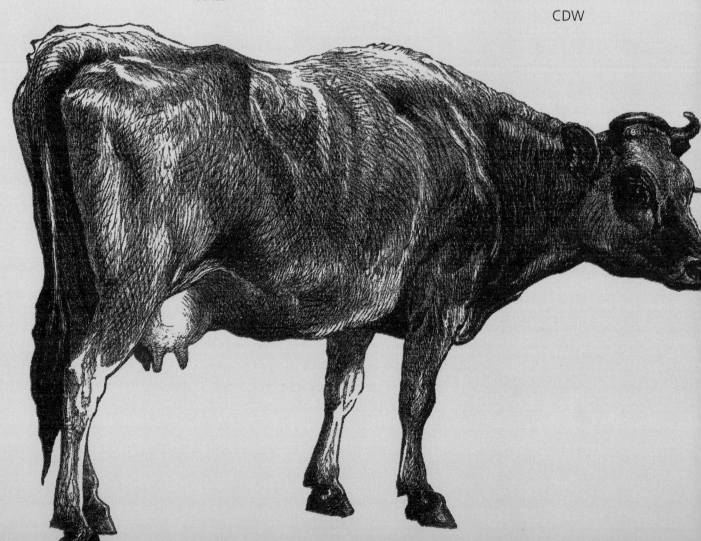

BEADLE PLUM CAKE

This is really rather a sneaky recipe to put in this chapter on butter, but you cannot make a large rich cake without lots of it.

450g/1lb butter, at room temperature
450g/1lb caster sugar
9 eggs
500g/1lb 2oz plain flour
2 tsp mixed spice
1¹/₂ tsp baking powder
225g/8oz raisins
225g/8oz currants
225g/8oz sultanas
115g/4oz chopped mixed peel
Grated zest and juice of 1 lemon

Cream the butter with the sugar until light and fluffy. Break the eggs into a bowl, set over a pan of hot water and whisk into the creamed mixture. Sift over the flour, spice and baking powder, and fold into the mixture. Add the raisins, currants, sultanas, mixed peel, and lemon zest and juice, and mix to a soft consistency.

Turn into a greased and lined 23–25cm/9–10in cake tin and smooth the top level. Bake in a preheated oven at 180°C/350°F/Gas 4 for about 2 hours.

BOSWORTH BUTTER JUMBLES

This recipe comes from Leicestershire, with the unlikely story that it was picked up on the battlefield of Bosworth where King Richard III's cook dropped it. They are however, delicious little biscuits.

175g/6oz unsalted butter, at room temperature
450g/1lb caster sugar
1 egg
225g/8oz plain flour

Cream the butter with the sugar until light and fluffy. Beat in the egg, then add the flour and mix to a stiff consistency.

Shape the dough into small 'S' forms and place on a greased baking tray. Bake in a preheated oven at 180°C/350°F/Gas 4 for 25 minutes or until golden.

Opposite: Beadle Plum Cake

BEURRE BLANC

This is the simplest and most magical of the kitchen sauces. There is no real reason why it should work, but it does work extremely well. Be painstaking and do not try rushing.

6 tbsp dry white wine
6 tbsp white wine vinegar
3 shallots, very finely chopped
Salt and freshly ground pepper
300g/10oz cold unsalted butter, diced

In a heavy stainless-steel or enamelled saucepan, boil the wine and vinegar with the shallots and a pinch of salt until only enough liquid remains to moisten the shallots. Remove the pan from the heat and allow to cool for a few minutes.

Season with pepper. Place the pan on a fireproof mat or flame diffuser over a very low heat. Whisk in the butter, a handful of dice at a time, until the sauce has a creamy consistency. Remove from the heat as soon as all the butter has been incorporated. You may find that you need a little more or a little less butter.

NOTE: Serve this sauce with the baked sea trout in the Salt chapter (page 13)

MAÎTRE D'HÔTEL BUTTER

This is Mappe Toulouse-Lautrec's version of the classic French maître d'hôtel butter. The well known cook was also the great-great niece of that well known artist. I like a lump of it served on top of a nice, juicy sirloin steak, although I usually put some garlic into the butter too. There are many different versions, and you can mess around until you find one you like. There are a lot of other savoury butters, including something called Parisian butter that contains 18 ingredients!

150g/5oz unsalted butter
1 tbsp finely chopped fresh tarragon
1 tbsp French mustard
Salt and freshly ground pepper
2 tsp lemon juice

Cream the butter with the back of a wooden spoon until smooth. Work in the finely chopped tarragon and the mustard. Salt and pepper lightly, and finally work in the lemon juice.

RHUBARB BARM BRACK

Barm brack, a tea bread made with tea, is also known in Ireland as St Brigid's bread. This is a slight variation on the theme because I have added a teaspoonful of bicarbonate of soda to lift the wholemeal flour.

175g/6oz soft brown or caster sugar

300g/10oz currants or mixed dried fruit

55g/2oz chopped mixed peel

600ml/1 pint freshly made tea, cooled and strained

1 egg, beaten

55g/2oz butter, softened

350g/12oz wholemeal flour

1 level tsp bicarbonate of soda

1 level tsp mixed spice

900g/2lb rhubarb, cut into 2.5cm/1in pieces

1 tsp sugar

Put the sugar, dried fruit and peel into a bowl and pour on the tea. Cover and leave to stand for at least 6 hours.

Add the beaten egg and softened butter to the fruit mixture and stir in. Sift in the flour, bicarbonate of soda and spice, and beat until smooth. Put into a greased and lined 1kg/2lb loaf tin. Bake in a preheated oven at 180°C/350°F/Gas 4 for 1½ hours or until well risen and firm to the touch. Turn out on to a wire rack and cool.

Put the rhubarb into a non-metallic saucepan with the 1 tsp sugar and a small amount of water. (If you do not want to use sugar with the rhubarb, a piece of angelica stalk will remove tartness from the fruit.) Poach the rhubarb for just a few minutes as you want to keep the pieces whole. Drain.

Pour the rhubarb over the tea bread (you could also pour the juice from the rhubarb over the top just before serving). Top with fresh cream, whipped if you prefer. As with all tea breads, it can also be eaten spread liberally with butter.

PEACHES

It has always puzzled me why it should be complimentary to describe a beautiful woman as having a complexion like peaches and cream. A nasty sight to behold it would be – yellow and white, more like some terrible disease. But I suppose if you pick a white peach, with its faint blush on almost white skin, from an espaliered tree in a walled garden on a lovely English summer's day, it could be recommended.

It is quite difficult to find the perfect peach, as they are often either too big and pappy within or pretending to be ripe with a nasty hard centre. But when they are at their very best, with a great flavour, they can be one of the best fruits in the world, as they have a slight tartness in the juicy but sweet flesh. A very small number of readers may live near an English peach orchard or a big house where walled peaches are still grown, and if you can obtain the fruits from there then you are to be envied. So make good use of the privilege. If you have peaches that are not quite as ripe as they should be, you can peel and slice them and then pour some boiling light sugar syrup over them – it cooks them just enough as it cools down. If the peaches are even harder, put them into the boiling syrup and bring it back to the boil before taking the pan from the stove. This kind of method is ideal for poaching rather tasteless fruits and yet not over-cooking them.

One of the famous peach dishes of our times is the rather (to my mind) dreadful Peach Melba, invented by Escoffier for the great singer Dame Nelly Melba. I find it rather sickly, with the vanilla ice-cream, raspberry sauce and, sometimes, raspberry jam. I infinitely prefer Peaches Cardinal, which has sieved raspberries poured over a whole poached peach and then a sprinkling of a few slices of blanched almonds – much better texture and taste. I used fresh basil as a garnish when I cooked this for the late Cardinal Basil Hume.

There is a nice story about Edward VII dining incognito with a young woman in Paris, as was his wont. When the bill came he was astounded at the price of the Montreuil peaches, famous in France for their lusciousness and flavour. He called the waiter over, saying 'Peaches must be very rare this year.' 'Ah, yes Sir,' replied the waiter. 'But not as rare as kings.' I don't think you can find those peaches anymore – the orchards have disappeared, and the big road to Charles De Gaulle airport runs through where they were.

JP

COLD CURRIED PEACHES

This makes a useful and easy starter for an informal meal.

4 large ripe peaches

For the sauce:
1 tbsp oil
2 tbsp chopped onion
1 clove of garlic, sliced
1 tbsp medium curry paste
2 tsp tomato purée
³/₄ tsp cayenne pepper
8oz tin tomatoes with the juice
1 tbsp red wine vinegar
1 tbsp lemon juice
2 tbsp water
Pinch of sugar
Salt and freshly ground pepper
1 tbsp lightly whipped double cream (approx)

To garnish:
Shredded lettuce
Chopped parsley
Paprika

To make the sauce, heat the oil over a medium heat, add the onion and garlic, and cook for 2–3 minutes. Add the curry paste, tomato purée and cayenne pepper, stir and cook for another 2–3 minutes. Add the remaining ingredients, except the cream, and bring to the boil, then simmer for 10 minutes.

Leave to cool, then purée the sauce in a blender. Taste and adjust seasoning if necessary. If the sauce is too thick, add a little extra lemon juice or water. When the sauce is cold, fold in the cream – the amount used depends not only on the consistency of the sauce, but on whether a milder flavour is desired.

Both the peaches and sauce should be very cold for serving. Skin the peaches and cut in half, discarding the stone. Place half a peach on each small plate and coat with the curry sauce. Add a little shredded lettuce to the side of the plate and decorate with a little chopped parsley and/or some paprika.

PEACH CHUTNEY

900g/2lb peaches, skinned
600ml/1 pint malt vinegar
(approx)
450g/1lb onions, chopped
225g/8oz sultanas
225g/8oz dark brown sugar
1¹/₂ tsp salt
³/₄ tsp ground cinnamon
1 tbsp mustard seed
2.5cm/1in cube of fresh root
ginger, peeled and finely
grated
Grated zest and juice of 1
large lemon

Cut up the peaches, discarding the stones, and place in a good aluminium pan, or, better still, a stainless steel preserving pan. (Copper pans should never be used for chutneys.) Pour over the vinegar – just enough to cover the fruit. Add the remaining ingredients and bring to the boil.

Lower the heat and simmer until a soft chutney consistency, bearing in mind that it will thicken slightly when cold and also if kept for any length of time. Stir the chutney frequently to prevent sticking.

When ready, pour into hot jars and seal immediately. As with most chutneys it is best kept a week or two before using.

BELLINI COCKTAIL

This is, without doubt, one of my very favourite cocktails. The peaches must be fresh and ripe, otherwise they are best omitted – which still leaves a delicious cocktail.

2–3 ripe peaches
Peach schnapps
Chilled sparkling wine or
champagne

Skin the peaches, remove the stones and purée the flesh in a blender. Sieve to obtain the juice.

Put 2 tbsp of peach juice and 2 tbsp of peach schnapps in a tall glass and stir well. Fill the glass with sparkling wine, stir once again and serve.

GRILLED PEACHES AND CREAM

4 medium-sized fresh ripe
 peaches
3–4 macaroons, crushed
1 level tbsp demerara sugar
1–2 tbsp Cointreau
For the topping:
300ml/¹/₂ pint double cream
150g/5oz demerara sugar

Pour boiling water over the peaches and leave for a minute or two, then pour off the water and cover them with cold water. The skins should then be easily removed. Halve the peaches, discarding stones, and place in a single layer in an ovenproof dish, cut sides up.

Mix the macaroons with the sugar and enough of the Cointreau to make a paste. Fill the peach cavities with the paste. If necessary the peach cavities can be made a little larger by removing some of the flesh, which should be finely chopped and added to the paste.

Whip the cream and spread over the peaches. Put the peaches to chill in the refrigerator.

When ready to serve, sprinkle demerara sugar over the cream and place under a preheated hot grill until the sugar melts.

NOTES & INDEX

1. SALT

Salt – otherwise sodium chloride – is actually an essential part of our body chemistry, required for the regulation of fluid balance. It is also one of the basic tastes that can be detected by the tongue. What it does is stimulate the taste-buds on the tongue to recognise the inherent flavour of a food, and in doing so enhances and sharpens that flavour. There are salts and salts though. We think the best is sea salt, which is literally evaporated from the sea. Rock salt is mined from the deposits of ancient, dried-up seas. Both these come in fine and coarse forms. The table salt most of us use in cooking and in salt cellars is a heavily refined type of salt, which contains additives to make it free-flowing.

2. PASTA

Pasta can be made or bought fresh, but there is a huge choice in packets of dried pastas from Italy. The best pastas are made from durum wheat, or 'hard' wheat flour; other pastas, made from softer wheats, tend to disintegrate during boiling to a gluey and sticky mass. A pasta made with durum flour will be dull rather than shiny, and slightly rough to the touch. Pasta aficionados say that you should only buy dried durum wheat pasta that has been formed in a proper metal mould, rather than a modern nylon or plastic one. The metal imparts that slight roughness which encourages sauces to stick to the pasta – the whole point of pasta! And always match your pasta shape to sauce: smooth and clinging sauces for smooth or slightly ridged shapes; thinner or lumpier sauces for pastas with deep ridges, curved shapes etc.

3. LOBSTER

The only trouble with lobster is cooking it, and for the flesh to be at its best, the lobster must be alive or very recently dead. This usually involves dispatching it yourself. The recommended ways of doing this have varied considerably over the years, but the RSPCA now believe that by freezing the lobster for about 2 hours, and then plunging it into boiling water or brine, the lobster will be dozy, numb and won't feel anything. And no, it's not cruel to put lobsters in the freezer, they live in very cold waters anyway. If you want to grill a lobster – in other words, use its flesh raw rather than boiled – we would freeze it as above then blanch it for a moment or so only.

4. BROAD BEANS

Broad beans are the first beans to appear in the spring, May and June in Britain. If you are a gardener, you can cook them pods and all when very young, but most of us can only get them when a bit older – but they are still delicious, so buy and cook as often as you can throughout that very short season. When cooking broad beans (or any other type of green bean), speed is of the essence. Plunge them into plenty of vigorously boiling, generously salted water, which will quickly return to the boil again. The salt will also raise the temperature of the water, again speeding up the cooking. And never cover the pan with a lid, as this will cause discoloration of the vegetable.

5. BEEF ON THE BONE

The banning of beef on the bone followed the horrors of BSE, which was the result of intensive farming, giving animals foods that were not natural in order to promote growth cheaply. We have now to acknowledge that the best beef – for which the British Isles have been famous for centuries – is never going to be cheap, and we must be prepared to pay for it. Much better to have the occasional expensive roast rib of beef as a treat, than indifferent beef more often, or indeed no beef at all.

6. CHICKEN

The key words to look for are 'traditional free-range'. You can be assured that the birds are not so intensively reared as 'battery' or 'barn' birds, are a little older – when the flavour improves – and have had access to grass as well as grain, and some sunlight, so have enjoyed their short lives more. The same applies to other poultry birds – the spring chickens or poussins, the plump capon (when you can find him), guinea fowl and quail, good old boiling fowl, and the turkey.

7. CHILLIES

It's curious that chilli peppers and capsicum or sweet peppers come basically from the same plant; sweet peppers are usually so bland. The heat of a chilli emanates from a chemical substance called capsaicin, and this is primarily concentrated in the ribs, or internal membranes, and the seeds. Capsaicin is not water soluble, which is why drinking water will not help counter heat. To prevent the capsaicin penetrating the pores of your skin when preparing chillies, rub your hands first with oil, or wear surgical gloves...

8. PARSLEY

To keep parsley fresh, sit the stems in a glass of water – but not for too long. Parsley can be washed in cold water, shaken half dry, then stored in the salad section in the fridge in a plastic bag. It could also be wrapped damp in paper kitchen towels in the fridge. Grow some yourself at home: even in a windowbox you can grow a plant big enough to cover most kitchen needs. The seeds are slow to germinate though, so be patient.

9. MUSTARD

Mustard seeds contain some 30-35 per cent of hot volatile oils, which is where the hot flavour of mustard is concentrated. The seeds have to be crushed and macerated in a warm liquid (once 'must', or new wine), before these oils can be released; the liquid must not be too hot, though, otherwise the oils will evaporate. For much the same reason, to preserve flavour and heat, made mustards are usually added to a dish towards the end of its cooking time.

10. OLIVES

If you have no choice but to buy olives bottled or jarred in brine, you can improve them at home. Drain them off, then rinse well to get rid of all traces of the salty brine. Put them in a sterile jar and cover them with olive oil. Add flavourings of choice – a sprig of thyme, a halved garlic clove, a few lightly crushed black peppercorns, some lemon peel or a small dried chilli – and leave for a few weeks. The flavour of the olives will be vastly improved, and you will have a very tasty olive oil to use in salad dressings.

11. SNAILS

When you collect your snails from field or garden, put them into a tray as already mentioned, or a box with sides. To prevent them escaping, put on a lid with several air-holes punched in it. Leave the snails without food for a couple of days of purging, or you could give them some oatmeal, lettuce or fennel herb to eat.

12. ANCHOVIES

These savoury little fish belong to the herring family, and there are various species around the world. The ones we see come mainly from the Mediterranean and the Atlantic around Spain, although shoals of the fish can be found as far north as Brittany. They are canned as fillets in brine and in oil, the latter infinitely preferable, and the larger tins are best from Spain. Salted anchovies are available too from delicatessens, sold by the gram from huge tins. These need to be washed free of salt and you could also soak them for an hour or so in milk or water. They come whole, so you must then remove the spines and heads. Use quickly, or they will discolour, or cover in olive oil if preparing in advance.

13. SAUSAGES

A sausage generally consists of ground meat, with or without fillers and flavourings, which is encased in a skin. The variety of sausages from around the world is enormous. They can be fresh like our own pork sausages or German Bratwurst; they can be dried and smoked like many French and German sausages; scalded and perhaps smoked, like chorizo and Frankfurters; or cooked and boiled, a category which can include black pudding. Incidentally, faggots, haslet and haggis are types of sausage, and in Aberdeen fish and chip shops you can find small black puddings and sausage-shaped haggises dipped in batter and deep-fried!

14. ROES

All fish produce roe, and that includes shellfish such as lobster (although lobster roe is usually known as coral). Most roes are edible, although that of certain members of the barracuda and puffer fish families is toxic. There are two categories of roe – soft and hard. It may surprise you to know that the soft cod's roe we commonly see is actually the milt or sperm of the male fish; the harder, more granular cod's roe is female fish eggs. Apart from the roes mentioned on pages 92-7, you could also try, at various seasons, and at various locations around the world, carp, mackerel, shad, flounder, haddock, perch, pike, coley, bleak and whitefish roes...

15. GARLIC

Fresh, new-season garlic appears in the spring. The heads are large, covered in a soft skin, and the 'meat' inside is still juicy, but the cloves are very difficult to peel. It is these self-same heads which are dried and are on sale throughout the rest of the year; the cloves slightly shrink, and the skin becomes the more familiar dry parchment casing. Always feel a head of garlic before buying: every clove should feel firm. To peel a clove, place on a board, and press on it hard with the blade of a knife; the skin can now be removed very easily. Try to remove any green central germ – the beginnings of a new shoot – as this can taste bitter.

16. OFFAL

In addition to careful cooking, offal needs careful preparation. Calf's liver needs the skin or surface membrane removed, as well as any fibrous connective tissue. Chicken, goose or duck livers should have any green-stained bits removed, as well as the gall bladder, for these will impart a bitter taste to any dish. Ox kidneys and liver would probably benefit from a brief soaking in milk to remove any bitterness, and any gristle should be cut away. Sweetbreads must be prepared as described on page 108.

17. CARDOONS

Cardoons are native to the Mediterranean, and belong to the same family as the globe artichoke. They grow as tall as artichokes, and have a similar prickly, multi-leaved head which develops into a purple thistle when mature. However, it is the leaf stalks of cardoon that are eaten, not the heads, and these are cultivated in much the same way as celery, blanched under earth to whiten and tenderise them. Only the inner stems and heart are eaten, so the stalks should be trimmed of roots, prickles and leaves. They are then cut into suitable lengths, and soaked, blanched or indeed cooked in acidulated water to prevent discoloration – or cooked in a 'blanc' (see page 113) which has the same effect. Well trimmed cardoons can be eaten raw, most famously with bagna cauda, the anchovy and garlic 'hot bath' of Piedmont.

18. OYSTERS

Native oysters are at their best in the winter, in the months with an R in them. It is during the summer that they reproduce, retaining their eggs or spat in their bodies, thus the unpleasant milkiness. Oysters must be bought live in the shell; the shells need to be tightly shut, or should shut briskly when tapped. If you must, store oysters in the fridge, which slows down their metabolism, but they are really best eaten as soon as possible. Plump oysters, with plenty of juices, should feel heavy and sound full, not empty, when you tap the shell.

19. PHEASANT

The season for pheasant runs from 1 October to 1 February, and the birds are best from October to January. Knowing the age of a bird is vital for the cook: young birds can be roasted, but older tougher birds will probably need to undergo longer cooking, in liquid. Their feet can be an indicator: those of older birds will be quite rough, scaly and calloused, while those of young birds will be soft and smooth. The large tail feather of young birds will be pointed rather than rounded. And all pheasants, bar those which have been badly shot, will benefit from a few days' hanging: the time will depend on the ambient temperature and indeed on personal taste.

20. CRAB

Once you've cooked your crab, you need to extract the meat. Do so by placing it on its back shell, then break off the claws and legs. Crack them open and dig out the white meat using a crab pick or skewer. To open the body, lift up and twist off the bony pointed flap or tail. Using your hands, or the point of a knife, push up and remove the central body section. Discard the soft gills – known as 'dead men's fingers' – from the sides, and then carefully and meticulously prise out the white meat from the cavities of the body, discarding any pieces of membrane and broken shell. Place all this sweet flesh in a bowl, then scrape out the brown meat left in the shell, and put in a separate bowl.

21. TRIPE

Tripe is the term used to collectively describe the four stomachs of ruminant or cud-chewing animals, usually beef. Without going into too much anatomical detail, the most common tripe types found are from the first stomach, the rumen, known as blanket tripe, and the second stomach, the reticulum, known as honeycomb tripe. The latter is tenderer. Tripe in Britain is cleaned, scraped, washed and scalded until snowy white, then soaked or marinated, and par-cooked before being sold. (Tripe on the Continent is sold prepared as well, but not cleaned to the point of whiteness.) The tripe is now to be cooked further.

22. EELS

The life cycle of the common eel is extraordinary, and only at the beginning of the twentieth century was the truth discovered. Eels are born and die in salt water, but spend their entire lives otherwise in fresh. Mature eels make their way from their home rivers in Europe and America and spawn in the deep Sargasso Sea, not far from Bermuda. Every spring thousands of tiny, transparent, worm-like baby eels, known as elvers, drift on the Gulf Stream back north and then swim, by some fantastic instinct, to the home rivers of their parents. In the case of the European eel, this involves a journey of some 3,000 miles, which can take up to three years. They make their way up river, diverting into streams and ponds (often wriggling across dry land to do so). There they mature and grow for five to seven years, before undertaking the journey back to the Sargasso Sea where they spawn and die...

23. SALMON

The salmon story is almost as romantic as that of the eel. Atlantic salmon live and feed off the coast of Greenland, and then swim back to their home European and American rivers to spawn. Having gorged themselves at sea in advance of the rigours of spawning, they are not tempted to eat when they are in fresh water, but that is where the skill of the salmon fisherman is truly revealed, in choosing just the right fly, casting in the most propitious direction...After spawning, some salmon make it back to the sea, but many die. The baby salmon or fry live in fresh water until at least a year old, sometimes three years, then return to the sea to feed, mature for two to three years, and then swim back to the rivers where they were born.

24. LAMB

Cuts from a baby lamb are easy to recognise, as the bones are very small, and the colour of the flesh, which is very pale, looks more like veal than lamb. A spring lamb will obviously be a bit bigger in size, and it should have a layer of white fat, some fat marbling the flesh, and a flesh that is deep pink in colour. A hogget or mutton, if you are lucky enough to find it, will have much darker flesh and creamier fat.

25. WALNUTS

Because of their oil content, most nuts, including walnuts, can easily turn rancid. Always buy nuts in their shells if possible, and make sure, especially with walnuts, that the shell is complete and not broken or cracked. The whiter the shell, the better the nut, so they say. Once shelled, or if you buy shelled walnuts, store them in the fridge or in a cool place in an airtight container. Ground or chopped nuts will spoil more quickly than whole nuts, and can completely ruin a dish in which they are used. Walnut oil reacts in the same way, so keep it in the fridge.

26. LEMONS

A good juicy lemon will feel heavy for its size, and should have a noticeably lemony smell. To maximise the juice, and make it easier to extract, roll the fruit quite firmly on a hard surface with the palm of your hand. Most lemons imported from abroad will have been coated in wax to prevent moisture loss, so if you want to use the zest – the outer layer of skin where the lemon oils are concentrated – wash the fruit well first in warm water.

27. FIGS

Figs belong to the same family as mulberries and breadfruit. Fresh figs, normally green, black or purple-red with a bloom, are available from early summer to autumn. They are ready to eat when slightly soft to the touch with a sweet odour. The 'flesh' inside is actually the flower of the tree, many tiny flowers fused together, and this is soft, red, sweet and fibrous with lots of tiny seeds. The best varieties are the Smyrna from Turkey, the black or dark purple mission fig from America and the Calimyrna, a hybrid of a native Californian variety and Smyrna.

28. COFFEE

As in many other strongly flavoured foods and flavourings, the essential oils are very volatile, so once ground, coffee beans should be used as soon as possible. For flavouring purposes, a dark roast is preferable to a light or medium. You can make your own coffee essence at home. Mix an equal volume of a good-quality, fine instant coffee and boiling water. Leave to cool and steep for a day or so before use. Or make coffee with grounds then strain and boil to reduce to the flavour required.

29. RASPBERRIES

Although they are so perishable when fresh, raspberries can be frozen very successfully. This is because they are what is known as a multiple fruit. As each tiny segment of a raspberry (or blackberry, mulberry etc) hides a hard seed, there is less watery flesh to break down during the freezing process. Choose perfect specimens, place them on a tray lined with freezer film, and open-freeze. When frozen, fold the film around them, secure shut, and return to the freezer. You can then enjoy them out of season – wonderful at Christmas, say!

30. CREAM

Seven types of cream are available in Britain, which vary in richness and fat content, so there really is no excuse not to include some in your cooking or eating. Half cream contains about 12 per cent fat; single about 18 per cent (and soured cream, which is made from single). Crème fraîche has at least 30 per cent fat, whipping cream some 35 per cent, and double cream has 48. Clotted, the richest of them all, has a fat content of 55 per cent. Only creams with a higher fat content, above 35 per cent, can be whipped or frozen.

31. CHOCOLATE

You must be very careful when melting chocolate. It must never be put over a direct heat unless it is accompanied by some liquid. It is best to put the broken-up, grated or chopped chocolate in a bowl that will fit over a saucepan of water without touching the water. Heat the water gently, and the steam on the base of the bowl will slowly melt the chocolate. If the steam or some water actually touches the chocolate, it will 'seize', and tighten into a mass that will melt. If this happens, add a very little cocoa butter, vegetable oil or clarified unsalted butter, a teaspoon at a time: the fat will make the chocolate smooth and pliable again.

32. APPLES

Apples have different cooking qualities. Cooking apples such as Bramleys are too sour to eat in the hand, but when cooked, they will melt to a sauce texture, the perfect accompaniment for roast pork or duck if spiked with some butter, a pinch of sugar and sweet spice and some lemon zest. Dessert apples such as Granny Smith or Braeburn can be cooked as a garnish as they keep their shape well. Try some apple rings or slices fried in butter with pork or duck, or some apple wedges caramelised in butter with sugar, finished with an apple liqueur, as an accompaniment to a pudding or ice-cream. And dessert apples can be eaten raw other than in the hand: they add crunch to salads (lovely with cold chicken, walnuts and celery), and a few wedges are magnificent with a piece of good Cheddar.

33. BUTTER

Butter usually consists of some 80 per cent butter fat and 20 per cent water and milk solids, or whey. It is the latter that can burn when butter is overheated, which is why butter is clarified when higher cooking temperatures are required. The butter is heated gently until the fat separates from the water and whey, and then the fat is carefully poured off, leaving the detritus at the bottom of the pan. Unsalted butter is the next best to use for high-heat cooking as its whey content is lower than salted; unsalted is also the most appropriate butter to use for light dessert pastries and puddings. Salted butter will last longer than unsalted, but because the salt acts as a preservative, this means that the whey content can be higher, so the butter will scorch more easily.

34. PEACHES

Peaches shipped in from abroad will have been picked before they are perfectly ripe, and so they will never be as sweet as if they'd been left on the tree. Sometimes it is best to buy imported peaches later on in the summer when they may well have had longer on the tree for their inimitable sweetness to develop. Peaches bought under-ripe may become softer at home, but they will never become sweeter.

RECIPE BREAKDOWN

NB: Illustrated recipes in italics

CAKES & BISCUITS & BREAD

MISCELLANEOUS

INDEX

NB: entries in bold type are names of recipes